CCCC STUDIES IN WRITING & RHETORIC
Edited by Steve Parks, University of Virginia

The aim of the CCCC Studies in Writing & Rhetoric (SWR) Series is to influence how we think about language in action and especially how writing gets taught at the college level. The methods of studies vary from the critical to historical to linguistic to ethnographic, and their authors draw on work in various fields that inform composition—including rhetoric, communication, education, discourse analysis, psychology, cultural studies, and literature. Their focuses are similarly diverse—ranging from individual writers and teachers, to work on classrooms and communities and curricula, to analyses of the social, political, and material contexts of writing and its teaching.

SWR was one of the first scholarly book series to focus on the teaching of writing. It was established in 1980 by the Conference on College Composition and Communication (CCCC) in order to promote research in the emerging field of writing studies. As our field has grown, the research sponsored by SWR has continued to articulate the commitment of CCCC to supporting the work of writing teachers as reflective practitioners and intellectuals.

We are eager to identify influential work in writing and rhetoric as it emerges. We thus ask authors to send us project proposals that clearly situate their work in the field and show how they aim to redirect our ongoing conversations about writing and its teaching. Proposals should include an overview of the project, a brief annotated table of contents, and a sample chapter. They should not exceed 10,000 words.

To submit a proposal, please register as an author at www.editorialmanager.com/nctebp. Once registered, follow the steps to submit a proposal (be sure to choose SWR Book Proposal from the drop-down list of article submission types).

SWR Editorial Advisory Board

Steve Parks, SWR Editor, University of Virginia
Kevin Browne, University of the West Indies
Ellen Cushman, Northeastern University
Laura Gonzales, University of Texas at El Paso
Haivan Hoang, University of Massachusetts–Amherst
Carmen Kynard, Texas Christian University
Paula Mathieu, Boston College
Staci M. Perryman-Clark, Western Michigan University
Eric Pritchard, University at Buffalo
Jacqueline Rhodes, Michigan State University
Tiffany Rousculp, Salt Lake Community College
Khirsten Scott, University of Pittsburgh
Jody Shipka, University of Maryland, Baltimore County
Bo Wang, California State University

Rhetorics of Overcoming
Rewriting Narratives of Disability and Accessibility in Writing Studies

Allison Harper Hitt
Ball State University

Conference on College
Composition and
Communication

National Council of
Teachers of English

National Council of Teachers of English
340 N. Neil St., Suite #104, Champaign, Illinois 61820
www.ncte.org

Staff Editor: Bonny Graham
Manuscript Editor: Susan Vargas-Sheltra
Interior Design: Mary Rohrer
Cover Design: Pat Mayer
Cover Image: Rachel Deane, "In Search for a Weapon I Found My Bonnard Book," Oil on Canvas, 40"×54", 2016. Rachel Deane is a California-based artist who utilizes her vivid visual memory to help her locate information sometimes lost through a learning difference that makes it difficult to recall words, names, and other small pieces of information. "In Search for a Weapon I Found My Bonnard Book" is based on a memory of contemplating using a Pierre Bonnard catalog as a defense mechanism in case she was assaulted. In the world of the painting, the book is being used as a literal weapon for physical safety, but in real life, the book provided Deane with valuable information about how to build images of everyday existence—Bonnard's paintings are often of domestic scenes—and an understanding that she uses images as a defense in her everyday life. The normative way of existing in society is scripted with certain types of learning and processing expectations, but Deane's choice to learn about herself and process the world through images reflects her reliance on methods outside the prescriptive expectation.

NCTE Stock Number: 41540; eStock Number: 41557
ISBN 978-0-8141-4154-0; eISBN 978-0-8141-4155-7

Copyright © 2021 by the Conference on College Composition and Communication of the National Council of Teachers of English.

All rights reserved. No part of this publication may be reproduced or transmitted in any form or by any means, electronic or mechanical, including photocopy, or any information storage and retrieval system, without permission from the copyright holder. Printed in the United States of America.

It is the policy of NCTE in its journals and other publications to provide a forum for the open discussion of ideas concerning the content and the teaching of English and the language arts. Publicity accorded to any particular point of view does not imply endorsement by the Executive Committee, the Board of Directors, or the membership at large, except in announcements of policy, where such endorsement is clearly specified.

NCTE provides equal employment opportunity (EEO) to all staff members and applicants for employment without regard to race, color, religion, sex, national origin, age, physical, mental or perceived handicap/disability, sexual orientation including gender identity or expression, ancestry, genetic information, marital status, military status, unfavorable discharge from military service, pregnancy, citizenship status, personal appearance, matriculation or political affiliation, or any other protected status under applicable federal, state, and local laws.

Every effort has been made to provide current URLs and email addresses, but because of the rapidly changing nature of the web, some sites and addresses may no longer be accessible.

Library of Congress Cataloging-in-Publication Data
Names: Hitt, Allison, author.
Title: Rhetorics of overcoming : rewriting narratives of disability and accessibility in writing studies / Allison Harper Hitt.
Description: Champaign, Illinois : National Council of Teachers of English, 2021. | Series: Studies in writing & rhetoric | Includes bibliographical references and index. | Summary: "Addresses the in/accessibility of writing classroom and writing center practices for disabled and nondisabled student writers, arguing that rewriting rhetorics of overcoming —the idea that disabled students must overcome their disabilities in order to be successful—as narratives of coming over is one way to overcome ableist pedagogical standards" —Provided by publisher.
Identifiers: LCCN 2021004729 (print) | LCCN 2021004730 (ebook) | ISBN 9780814141540 (trade paperback) | ISBN 9780814141557 (adobe pdf)
Subjects: LCSH: Composition (Language arts)—Study and teaching. | English language—Rhetoric—Study and teaching. | English language—Remedial teaching. | Students with disabilities.
Classification: LCC LC4028 .H57 2021 (print) | LCC LC4028 (ebook) | DDC 371.9/044—dc23
LC record available at https://lccn.loc.gov/2021004729
LC ebook record available at https://lccn.loc.gov/2021004730

*To the women who shaped me—
my mom, especially*

CONTENTS

Acknowledgments   ix

1. Introduction: Rhetorics of Overcoming   1
2. (De)Valuing Disability: Moving beyond Accommodation Approaches to Accessibility in Writing Studies   34
3. Resisting Diagnosis and Creating Avenues for Agency in the Writing Center   61
4. Guaranteeing Access(ibility) in the Multimodal Writing Classroom   85
5. Conclusion: Toward an Ethics of Accessibility   122

Notes   131
Works Cited   137
Index   151
Author   159

ACKNOWLEDGMENTS

This book is a combination of many types of knowing and meaning-making—both an intellectual exploration of how writing studies has shaped and been shaped by disability discourses and a critical call for centering the body in both pedagogical and research environments. The challenge of navigating this process while struggling with my own mental and chronic health issues has at times felt insurmountable, and many people have supported me as I have slowly and clumsily come to terms with what sometimes feel like fractured parts of who I am as a person, instructor, and scholar.

This project emerged from my doctoral work, and it found its first form as a dissertation. To my mentors and codirectors, Lois Agnew and Patrick Berry, who provided me with pages of careful, conscientious, and critical feedback on the work that informed the ideas in this book: I am so grateful for your support and guidance, from assisting with my coursework and dissertation to visiting me in the hospital (and after, taking me to get ice cream) to offering advice as I transitioned into my first tenure-track position.

There have been so many folks who helped shape early ideas, theories, and drafts. I am always in awe of the calm brilliance of Collin Brooke, who talked through ideas over coffee. To Jay Dolmage, your teaching style, constructive feedback, and powerful scholarship have been so vital to me. From sitting in your office as a brand-new TA asking if it was okay that I had cried in front of my first-year writing students, to working with you on conference presentations and receiving your feedback on publications, I have found your mentorship invaluable. To Margaret Price, thank you for your thoughtful comments on the blog posts that fed into this project, your friendship, and your scholarship. When I first read *Mad at School*, I felt seen and assured that I don't have to fracture myself into discrete parts and keep my madness a secret.

I am grateful to everyone who shaped my graduate experience. Brian Ballentine, Nathalie Singh-Corcoran, and Scott Wible introduced me to the discipline through the professional writing and editing program at West Virginia University. To Scott, thank you for introducing me to the field and for assigning the book *A Rhetoric of Risk*, which helped me see for the first time how my background (growing up in coal country and watching young men being recruited out of high school to work in the mines) connected to my interests in professional writing. During my time at Syracuse, I took courses in the disability studies program that introduced me to disability not just as personal embodiment but also as a discipline and movement that is deeply intellectual, political, and grounded in activism and liberation. Thank you to Beth Ferri, whose classes transformed my understanding of what *matters* to me as an academic—and instructor. The folks in the composition and cultural rhetoric program had a profound impact on my PhD experience, so a special thanks to my peers: Jana Rosinski, Kate Navickas, Seth Davis, Jason Luther, Nicole Gonzales Howell, Karrieann Soto Vega, Lindsey Banister, Missy Watson, Rachael Shapiro, Tim Dougherty, LaToya Sawyer, Ben Kuebrich, Jason Markins, Melissa Kizina Motsch, Carolyn Ostrander, and Tamara Issak.

As a teacher, I first stepped into a classroom fresh out of college and still in the throes of grief from my mom's death only a few months before. I have been overwhelmed with gratitude over the years for how accepting and supportive my students have been with my madness, respecting that I sometimes need to communicate in alternative formats, bring my support dog to class, and prioritize taking time to care for myself. So thank you to all my students—first at WVU, then Syracuse, the University of Central Arkansas, and Ball State. Teaching you and learning with and from you has been an honor.

I owe many thanks to the folks behind the SWR series. To my editor, Steve Parks, thank you for the Skype calls, feedback, encouragement, and patience as I navigated this process in crip time. Writing a book while teaching four classes a semester was both humbling and exhausting. Trying to find energy to write about disability, overcoming narratives, and accessibility was even more difficult as I moved from diagnosis to diagnosis with overcoming discourses constantly engulfing me. Steve's patience between drafts and updates, with seemingly no frustration, was crucial for me to be able to finish this book. I am lucky to have had Stephanie Kerschbaum read these chapters. Stephanie, your work has been so important to my own, and your commitment to accessibility has been a constant source of inspiration (no, not *that* kind of inspiration). This book wouldn't be what it is without your careful, detailed feedback and our informal think-sessions at CCCC.

I am forever grateful for my family members who have embraced and accommodated difference. Thank you to my older brother, who taught me a lot as we grew up about how people perceive and respond to disability, and how to suspend judgment of others. To my dad, who supported me many years ago when I was diagnosed with depression, and who later stepped into the role of both parents, thank you. Academic life has taken me all over the country, and I am grateful that you are always a phone call away. To my mom, Susie, who encouraged me to apply for graduate school, I would not be here without you. Your advocacy and love of teaching influenced me more than I could ever express. When I read the letters from your former students, I knew I wanted to be the type of academic who advocates for and with folks whose voices are marginalized, ignored, and suppressed. I wish you could read this.

To my Pap, who was so excited that his English-major granddaughter was finally writing a book, you must be smiling somewhere. To my Gramma, my biggest supporter throughout my PhD (who later insisted on calling me Dr. Allie), I miss you every day.

Finally, to Rick: Thank you for encouraging me not to give up, for taking care of me every time I am too sick or depressed to eat, and for always being by my side. I am grateful to know and love you.

1

Introduction: Rhetorics of Overcoming

> Sometimes disabled people overcome specific moments of ableism—we exceed low expectations, problem-solve lack of access, avoid nursing homes or long-term psych facilities, narrowly escape police brutality and prison. However, I'm not sure that overcoming *disability* itself is an actual possibility for most of us. Yet in a world that places extraordinary value in cure, the belief that we can defeat or transcend body-mind conditions through individual hard work is convenient. Overcoming is cure's backup plan.
>
> —Eli Clare, *Brilliant Imperfection: Grappling with Cure*

I BEGIN, AS I USUALLY do when discussing disability, with a series of disclosures.

One. On the first day of every new class I teach, I disclose some version of the following to my students:

> My mom was sick with cancer the entire four years I was in college, and I had an agreement with the dean of my university that I could miss class or take extra time if I needed it. At the beginning of each semester for four years, I had to inform my professors of this arrangement. I know that you all have complicated lives beyond this class, and I don't require that you share them with me, but I do ask that you be mindful of our time together and let me know whenever possible if you will miss class or are unable to meet a deadline. I can work with you in restructuring due dates—*but only if you let me know you need help.*

I did not use this accommodation much (which is a different series of disclosures), but it attuned me to the idea of university accommodations—something that I saw peers struggle to obtain. And later, as I moved through different universities and learned about their accommodation systems, I realized what the dean had offered me was by no means a formal accommodation; it was informal, based not on proof of diagnosis but on a personal and institutional commitment to help a struggling student.

Two. In the final semester of my PhD program, I disclosed to a peer that I had/have a history of major depression and suicidal ideation—a risky disclosure that frequently requires reporting within university institutional spaces. I was told that this information was inappropriate to share in that space—a social function that I hosted at my house.

Three. In 2017, my doctors agreed that I needed a support animal to accompany me to work. She was *not* a service animal, and my university did not have a formal system in place for accommodating disabled faculty, which made the process difficult to navigate but also gave me some flexibility in what constituted *reasonable* accommodation. After an extended back-and-forth with the Disability Resource Center and Human Resources, the head of Human Resources contacted the Office of General Counsel, and I was granted permission for my support animal to be on campus: in my office, the classroom, and both departmental and university meetings. While my mental health often affects my ability to focus, speak, or engage in the classroom—and I try to have honest conversations about mental health with my students—these disabilities are otherwise invisible. Having a dog on campus, however, made it much more visibly clear to my students that there was *something* different about me without me needing to disclose anything. One morning, my students were talking about support animals as they waited for me to unlock the classroom. As my key entered the lock, a student said, "What do I need to do? Just pretend to be suicidal?"

These disclosures are surely familiar to folks with disabilities who have sought personal, professional, and institutional support. Often such disclosures are met with follow-up demands for specific diagnosis: *What happened to you that you need a support animal?* These questions are also accompanied by dismissal or counter-diagnoses. For example, a colleague once entered my office after reading a blog post I had written about a student calling me insane. They placed their hands on my desk, leaning their body forward to demand a diagnosis, which prompted an uncomfortable disclosure. They seemed relieved by the information: "Oh, that's not so bad. My son has [x], [y], *and* [z], which is way worse."

Why do these disclosures matter—individually and together? How do they create a picture of the complexities of disclosure in the writing classroom and in our professional and interpersonal spaces more broadly? How do such disclosures shape my ethos as a scholar and instructor with a variety of mental illness diagnoses? What role do such disclosures have in *this* space, in *this* discussion of rhetorics of overcoming disability?

PAYING ATTENTION TO DISABILITY

Disability has always been a lens through which I have viewed and understood people and environments, my family, and myself. In "Integrating Disability, Transforming Feminist Theory," Rosemarie Garland-Thomson describes disability as "the most human of experiences, touching every family and—if we live long enough—touching us all" (17). Similarly, in her foundational text, *Claiming Disability: Knowledge and Identity*, Simi Linton describes disability as a central tenet of the humanities that those of us working in higher education must critically address. Yet despite the scholarship that constructs disability as an intersectional and pervasive identity category, many people understand it within personal contexts: they or someone close to them has a disability. Michael Bérubé addresses this personal influence in the foreword to *Claiming Disability*:

> Part of the reason I changed my mind so dramatically has nothing to do with anything I've read; when I became the father of a child with Down syndrome, I realized immediately and viscerally that disability can happen to anyone—including someone very close to you, and including you, too. (x)

Disability has been woven into my family tapestry. Growing up with an autistic brother, I saw him pass through many different systems: speech, occupational, and music therapy; inclusive and special education classrooms; and disabled student and adult worker programs that are constantly in a state of political and financial flux. Disability was always around me, but I never thought critically about it until I saw others denied access to education and services and experienced disability myself. I often witnessed the discrimination my brother faced from neighbors, strangers at the grocery store, peers, and administrators. I watched as he shifted from an inclusive classroom environment in junior high school to a special education program in high school, where he was repeatedly denied access to social interactions with students outside the program and gradually became nonverbal. My mom's nondisabled status shifted suddenly when she was diagnosed with advanced-stage ovarian cancer that—after four years of chemotherapy and radiation treatments—prevented her from sitting, walking, and eventually feeding herself. As a young adult, my own nondisabled status shifted when I was first diagnosed with major depressive disorder and generalized anxiety disorder. Although disability was central to my childhood and early education, it only became visible to me once I witnessed and experienced the structural barriers and cultural stigma that denied members of my family access to educational, professional, and material resources.

These family experiences were all marked by narratives that implied we needed to overcome our different issues. For example, the emphasis on overcoming has been ever-present throughout my brother's medical history: a new diagnosis, a new form of therapy, a new treatment, new medications. "How do you think your brother would feel about being contained in an oxygen chamber?" my grandfather asked every time we spoke on the phone for a year. It was another new treatment—something he had read about in a magazine. When my mom had breast cancer during my early childhood, she was celebrated for overcoming—for *winning the battle* with cancer. And as many people with mental illnesses know (#ThingsDisabledPeopleKnow), there are constant messages urging them to overcome: *Mental issues are only a mindset, and overcoming them is a matter of strength, a demonstration of willpower. Have you tried yoga? Meditation? Exercise?* Overcoming narratives are all around us, pressuring nonnormative bodies to perform normalcy.

Disability frequently shapes and is shaped by personal relationships, but it is also culturally pervasive—shaped by media representations and medical discourses that present disability diagnoses as increasing, something to fear or overcome. We are a society that likes to diagnose and label, so these statistics about increasing diagnoses carry great significance for how we understand and respond to disability. In March 2014, the Centers for Disease Control and Prevention (CDC) reported that the proportion of children with a diagnosed autism spectrum disorder in the United States had increased from 1 in 88 to 1 in 68, a 30 percent increase ("CDC Estimates"). As of 2018, the CDC cites the number as 1 in 59; however, this statistic is based on just one study of 8-year-old children ("Data"). Autism is frequently referred to as a crisis, and framing data in a way that makes it appear more prevalent reinforces the fear of rapidly increasing rates. Disability is and has always been present. One in four adults in the United States has a disability ("CDC: 1 in 4"). One in six children has a developmental disability, such as autism, attention deficit disorder (ADD) or attention deficit hyperactivity disorder (ADHD), cerebral palsy, or an intellectual disability (Boyle et al.). These numbers should not alarm us; rather, they help contextualize the need for greater awareness and understanding of a significant portion of the population who are frequently marginalized; socially, economically, and physically mistreated; and misrepresented and exploited in research and through media representations.

These disability statistics have been documented in the context of higher education as well. According to the National Center for Education Statistics, 19 percent of undergraduate college students reported having a disability in 2015–2016 ("Fast Facts"). As in the larger population, this number includes individuals with physical, learning, and mental disabilities. In 2010, The John William Pope Center for Higher Education Policy (now The James G. Martin

Center for Academic Renewal) reported that 2 percent of college students had a documented learning disability, such as ADD, ADHD, or dyslexia (Vickers). Attention to disability in higher education has focused considerably on learning disabilities, but educational researchers have increasingly attended to the rates of undergraduate and graduate students with mental disabilities in higher education, and whether these student populations are supported and appropriately accommodated. In its 2015 annual report, the Center for Collegiate Mental Health reported that the number of college students seeking mental health services had grown at five times the rate of enrollment: from 2010 to 2015, "institutional enrollment grew by 5.6%, the number of students seeking services increased by 29.6%, and the number of attended appointments increased by 38.4%" (*Center for Collegiate Mental Health 2015* 7). In 2017–2018, 54.4 percent of students attended counseling for mental health concerns (*Center for Collegiate Mental Health 2018* 10). It isn't reasonable to speculate that this is solely because of an increase in disability; instead, this indicates a variety of factors, including a rise in diagnosis of mental health issues, a reduction in the stigma of counseling, and the availability of more support services. More urgently, these numbers indicate a need for more transparent conversations about mental illness in higher education. According to the 2013 National College Health Assessment, more than one-third of US college students had difficulty functioning due to depression, and 30 percent reported serious considerations of suicide—up from 24 percent in 2010 (Novotney). For four years, I taught 80 students per semester, and these statistics indicate that roughly 27 of my students *every semester* may have been struggling academically because of depression and suicidal ideation. These numbers are especially important to consider when structuring the pedagogical environments of writing centers and first-year writing classes that serve all university students regardless of their disciplines, expertise, or abilities.

Despite statistics of increasing diagnoses saturating our news and media, the purpose of this book is not to measure the validity of these increases or to determine whether there is a disability or mental health crisis in higher education. It is against and within this landscape, though, that this book exists because scientific, cultural, and personal discourses inform how we theorize and accommodate disability. Some education scholars argue that increasing cases of disability may simply indicate an increase in labels. For example, in *Now You See It: How the Brain Science of Attention Will Transform the Way We Live, Work, and Learn*, education scholar and innovator Cathy Davidson discusses cognition, active learning, and technology's ability to reimagine classroom practices and accommodate a diverse range of twenty-first-century learners. This reimagining is necessary, she notes, because we are more likely to label a student as learning disabled if they do not fit into our pedagogical practices (10). In other words, we diagnose, label, and accommodate—trying to fix our students rather than trying to fix our practices. As a writing professor, I am interested in how disability is positioned as something that must be diagnosed and overcome in order for disabled student writers to be successful. More specifically, as a mentally disabled writing professor, I am interested in practices that make college writing spaces more accessible to a wide range of students—and instructors—who do not identify as disabled, disclose disabilities, or seek institutional accommodations.

There is a persistent tendency in higher education to try to diagnose disabled students[1] and default to accommodations rather than crafting more accessible pedagogical environments. As in medicalized approaches to disability that rely on cure, disabled students are told to overcome their disabilities. In this way, overcoming becomes cure's backup plan. *Rhetorics of Overcoming: Rewriting Narratives of Disability and Accessibility in Writing Studies* has two interconnected aims: (1) to identify and analyze rhetorics of overcoming within the field of writing studies that have shaped disciplinary understandings of disability and writing; and (2) to develop strategies for overcoming ableist pedagogical expectations that are informed both by theories of multimodality[2] and disability studies (DS), and by the embodied needs of students. While this book is grounded in the field of writing studies and rhetoric, rhetorics of overcoming are not unique to this discipline; rather, these desires for diagnosing and overcoming disability extend far beyond college writing students. In this introduction, I define rhetorics of overcoming—disability discourses of diagnosis, disclosure, accommodation, and individual achievements—and illustrate how they operate within both public and academic discourses.

DEFINITIONS AND DISCOURSES OF OVERCOMING

The overcoming narrative is a classic trope in DS that positions disability as something that must be overcome for an individual to be successful—the disability version of the bootstraps narrative that individualizes struggles and achievements and glorifies triumph over personal hardships. Simi Linton argues that the overcoming narrative stems from ableist ideologies that position disability and disabled groups as inferior to able-bodied groups. Linton explains, "The popular phrase *overcoming a disability* is used most often to describe someone with a disability who seems competent and successful in some way, in a sentence something like 'She has overcome her disability and is a great success'" (17). This idea can be interpreted a couple of different ways: an individual has willfully risen above the limitations of their disability, or they have risen above society's expectations of how a disabled person should act and be. Most often, we encounter the first example: a woman who wills herself to walk again after a car accident, a boy with Down syndrome who makes the basketball team, a dyslexic student who overcomes her learning disability and gets a full ride to Harvard.

The ideology embedded in the overcoming narrative communicates "personal triumph over a personal condition" (Linton 18). That is, disability is an individual issue that requires individual attention. As Linton notes, this rhetoric has not been generated within the disability community; rather, it is an external demand from an ableist society that positions disability as something in need of cure. Often, this external demand is internalized. For example, a dyslexic student may be repeatedly told—because she transposes words or letters in her writing—that she is a bad writer, which she internalizes and carries into the college writing classroom. Writing instructors know that writing is more than grammar and usage, but the logic of overcoming demands that this student overcome the characteristics of dyslexia to be a successful writer.

The logic of overcoming disability exists in many contexts beyond the classroom, ranging from personal experiences to media representations of overcoming adverse issues with the body.[3] Although there are many examples of narratives of overcoming, I focus on those that have manifested in my own personal and social experiences: discourses of overcoming cancer, inspirational narratives circulated in print and digital media, and examples of academic ableism. My personal connection to these issues will be self-evident. These brief examples provide a starting point for understanding the wide-ranging manifestation of overcoming narratives, and I highlight how these discourses affect societal perceptions of disability before introducing how I use the term *coming over* to assess and reimagine more accessible writing pedagogies.

Discourses of Overcoming Cancer

For those who have experienced cancer or witnessed a loved one's experiences, the metaphor of cancer as a fight or battle is a familiar one. In her discussion of breast cancer, Kristen Garrison argues that in the cancer-as-war metaphor, "Women are enlisted in a battle against the self, their bodies made war zones, with cancer as the enemy, medical professionals as infallible heroes, and treatments of search-and-destroy by any means possible."[4] When my mom was dying, I listened to doctors, family members, neighbors, and grocery store acquaintances place responsibility on her to push through, to fight, to overcome because she was *too strong* to let cancer beat her. How we write about cancer, how we name and describe it, influences cultural and personal understandings. For example, as Karen Kopelson argues, "the language we use to talk about breast cancer makes possible or impossible what we understand, and then do, about breast cancer as the public, political, raced, classed, and gendered health crisis that it is" (131). The language of breast cancer often reduces the experience to the individual level rather than acknowledging the structures and intersectional differences that affect people's experiences.

Although I do not intend to conflate cancer and disability, there are similarities in their narratives about overcoming bodily issues. People with cancer may face long-term disabilities and, even if a person with cancer doesn't identify as disabled, their condition may be disabling (American Cancer Society). Jay Dolmage and Cynthia Lewiecki-Wilson contend that "any body subjected to the medical gaze becomes disabled to some extent, through its positioning as passive object, and through the over-signification of bodily deviation" (29). Narratives about cancer and disability share medicalized desires for diagnosis and cure for the abnormal body—the need for early detection, prevention, and technological intervention. There are overlaps, too, in the emphasis on overcoming adversity through determination and personal success. Breast cancer is an enterprise: it became the most common cancer worldwide in 2021 ("Cancer"), one in eight US women is diagnosed with it (*Breast Cancer Facts*), and millions of dollars are raised each year to research it.[5] It affects women and men regardless of race, class, age, or sexual identity, yet it is commercialized as an individual issue and as something that happens because someone was not proactive or happy or strong enough.

Narratives and rhetorics of overcoming cancer are everywhere. They manifest in the barrage of pink merchandise in October and the assurance that, when you buy a pale-pink can opener, you contribute five cents to Komen for the Cure. They are promoted in campaigns like #NoMakeupSelfie that purport to raise cancer awareness while erasing the experiences of individuals who undergo chemotherapy and radiation treatments.[6] They are represented on billboards on the side of the interstate—such as one that read, "Threw cancer a curve ball. Overcoming. Pass it on" ("Threw"). The image featured a young boy with one leg dressed in a baseball uniform and promoted the idea that if *I* can overcome cancer, so can *you*. Images like this are meant to be inspirational but also convey a message that we must try harder to overcome, that overcoming is as simple as "throwing a curve ball." Decontextualized representations about overcoming can do more harm than good, both to readers who come to expect and demand overcoming and to the folks such inspirational narratives purport to help.

Inspirational Discourses of Overcoming

In her discussion of the visual rhetorics of disability, Rosemarie Garland-Thomson ("Politics") categorizes and historicizes the ways in which images have worked to construct our understandings of disability. Images are powerful because of their immediacy, and Garland-Thomson argues, "Photography's immediacy, claim to truth, and wide circulation calcifies the interpretations of disability embedded in the images, at once shaping and registering the public perception of disability" (58). Images represent disability as wondrous, sentimental, exotic, or realistic. Overcoming invokes both wonder and sentimentality, which work together to "produc[e] the convention of the courageous overcomer, contemporary America's favorite figure of disability" (61). I contend that these inspirational messages—which can be found in many forms of both print and digital media—construct a societal expectation of individual responsibility to overcome, which ignores larger systems of inaccessibility and ableism that require people to "overcome" in order to be perceived as successful. These external demands and expectations for overcoming are harmful both to disabled individuals and to the possibilities of intervening in these inaccessible systems and rewriting more accurate, inclusive, and accessible narratives of disability.

The billboard example of Adam Bender, the young baseball player who threw cancer a metaphorical curve ball ("Threw"), exists within a larger narrative of overcoming adversity through a national campaign of inspirational messages funded by The Foundation for a Better Life (FBL). FBL is a nonprofit that provides motivational and inspirational messages "as a contribution toward promoting good values, good values and a better life" ("About Us"). FBL's advertisements feature positive values like equality, justice, and respect by highlighting the achievements of famous actors and actresses, professional athletes, humanitarians, and everyday Americans. In addition to television and radio commercials, FBL creates billboards as part of its commitment to public service: "The messages, depicting heroes of our time, are seen across America's highways and on Times Square. Thousands of schools around the world also use our motivational materials to communicate positive values to youth" ("About Us"). FBL constructs rhetorics of overcoming within cultural and educational contexts through its visual representations of overcoming, hard work, and determination. Indeed, Alison Kafer illustrates this in *Feminist, Queer, Crip*, drawing attention to FBL's circulation of ableist narratives that "prais[e] individuals with disabilities for having the strength of character to 'overcome' their disabilities" (87) and position overcoming as a way to live a *better* life.

Overcoming is often attributed to hard work and determination, and FBL represents "hard work" with an image of Whoopi Goldberg with the text "Overcaem dyslexia." The letters *e* and *m* are transposed as they might appear to a dyslexic reader. Emphasizing this writing error suggests the understanding that overcoming a disability does not erase a disability, but Goldberg's description still ends with a reminder to work hard: "Today, Goldberg has come a long way from a teenage mother to one of the most powerful women in show business, thanks to hard work—including the hard work of believing in herself" ("Overcaem"). Dyslexic students are often told that they are not determined or working hard enough to overcome their writing issues in the course of a semester, and messages like this emphasize the individual responsibility of working hard to overcome your disability.

FBL's billboards also include examples of academic determination, such as Harvard graduate Brooke Ellison smiling in her graduation robe and cap, with her wheelchair and ventilator visible. The text reads, "Quadriplegic. A-. Harvard." The image communicates a connection between Ellison's physical disability—a spinal injury from childhood—and her intellectual capacity. The fuller description details her high SAT scores and the role of her mother, who lived with her in the Harvard dormitories, but again Ellison's description ends with an inspirational message about determination: "No matter what sort of adversity or challenge you might face, you can always believe that, with hope, it can be conquered and, in the end, you will be stronger for it" ("Quadriplegic"). Each story of hard work and determination highlights willpower, inner strength, and the power of believing in yourself rather than acknowledging the importance of strong support networks or even suggesting that you do not need to erase your disability to succeed. Kafer writes, "Within this individualist framework, disability is presented as something to overcome through achievement and dedication" (89). Collectively, these advertisements are meant to inspire viewers to achieve their dreams; however, they also communicate a message about disability as something that must be overcome to reach those goals, which shuts down any possibilities of affirming disability as a positive attribute or way of being.

Many popular representations of disability invite overcoming and sentimental narratives, and these are common in both print and digital media. The overcoming narrative is widely circulated through inspirational news stories in forums like Reddit, YouTube, and other social media platforms. These stories are meant to inspire individuals to persevere and overcome their hardships—to make nondisabled readers feel happy that disabled people are overcoming adversity, guilty for not doing enough to accomplish our own goals, relieved that we are not them, or hopeful that we, too, can overcome if we find ourselves in a similar situation. For example, the Scott Hamilton quote "The only disability in life is a bad attitude" is frequently placed on images of physically disabled children or athletes. Images that encourage overcoming perpetuate medical-model views about disability, though in ways that are frequently well-intentioned. Disability activist Laura Hershey argues that we are hesitant to challenge or outright critique efforts that seem "fundamentally good, or at least well-meaning." At the same time, Hershey notes that the "actions which are intended to help a certain group of people *may actually harm* them" by reinforcing their devalued status. Images that encourage overcoming are intended to inspire but have damaging consequences.

Ultimately, overcoming narratives are meant to soothe the able-bodied, to make viewers feel better or be thankful for their bodies. Examples from Autism Speaks, an organization with a controversial mission and approach to raising awareness about autism, are seemingly endless. In 2015, Autism Speaks shared the article "They told my parents I wouldn't talk; Now I'm graduating from college" on its Facebook page with the following description: "This story of overcoming the obstacles will make your night. #AutismAwareness." The post got 10,460 reactions. I genuinely love stories like this. Many autistic people—my brother included—are able to accomplish much more than what doctors, therapists, and teachers predict. However, in very few words, this post invokes wonder (*Can you believe this?*) and self-indulgence by emphasizing how *readers* will feel after consuming this narrative. The circulation of inspirational overcoming narratives contributes to a cultural narrative of disability that is disembodied from disabled experiences and conflates overcoming with success. The saturation of these narratives about students overcoming their disabilities shapes assumptions and understandings of disability, who disabled students are, and what they need.

Disability Discourses in Higher Education: #AcademicAbleism
The social and cultural pervasiveness of rhetorics of overcoming necessarily influences how people understand and engage with disability in other contexts. In *Academic Ableism: Disability and Higher Education*, Jay Dolmage investigates the many ways in which university systems have been structured to exclude nonnormative bodies, minds, and abilities. Academic ableism is disability-based discrimination that occurs in higher education, and Dolmage argues that "the ethic of higher education still encourages students and teachers alike to accentuate ability, valorize perfection, and stigmatize anything that hints at intellectual (or physical) weakness" (3). Disabled students face physical, social, and pedagogical barriers that deny them equitable access to learning. Instructors know that students enter the classroom with a range of abilities, knowledges, and needs, but it can be difficult to create accessible pedagogical spaces when students' needs are not disclosed—either informally or institutionally.

In higher education, there is an expectation for students and instructors to overcome mental and psychiatric disabilities. Disability disclosures of mental illness are risky in academia, where we are "often still devoted to the mythos of the good man speaking well, the professor as bastion of reason, the *cogito ergo sum*" (Pryal 8).

In academia, where the mind is highly valued, there is fear among both students and faculty of disclosing any variations of the mind. The mentally disabled are often stripped of rhetorical significance and denied personhood, dismissed as rhetorically *un*sound. Margaret Price writes, "To lack rhetoricity is to lack all basic freedoms and rights, including the freedom to express ourselves and the right to be listened to" (*Mad* 26–27). There is an association and conflation of mental health with madness that necessitates a static notion of rationality for the rhetor to exist. Reflecting on her own psychiatric disability, Pryal writes, "I feared I would be seen as unreasonable, irrational, and therefore unable to do the work required of a professor. I feared that because of my disability, my career would be over" (4).

This fear of disclosure and retribution is widespread among faculty with psychiatric and mental disabilities. In a cross-institutional qualitative study of 267 mentally disabled university faculty, Margaret Price et al. reported that most of their survey respondents (86.9 percent) did not request accommodations from Disability Services, and many indicated fear that these requests "might affect tenure and promotion, lead to avoidance or poor treatment by others, or affect factors such as salary or job security." Narratives of mental illness in higher education emphasize deficit, discouraging disclosure by faculty members and, frequently, students.

Thousands of these narratives about ableism, mental illness, and higher education can be found on Twitter through the hashtag #AcademicAbleism. Taken together, these tweets contextualize how rhetorics of overcoming are written, circulated, and rewritten within academic contexts. From March 20, 2014, to December 30, 2018, there were roughly 2,300 #AcademicAbleism tweets. In the grand scheme of the Twittersphere, two thousand tweets in four years is not particularly noteworthy, but the hashtag has become a space used consistently by students and faculty to share everyday experiences with barriers in higher education, respond to cultural or popular discourses about disability in higher education, and advocate for accessible pedagogical and curricular practices. Perhaps most important, it has prompted a series of additional hashtags to continue the conversation about ableism in academic spaces.

The #AcademicAbleism hashtag emerged in March 2014 after *The Guardian* published multiple articles about graduate student mental health in a series titled "Mental Health: A University Crisis." These articles focus on how commonplace mental health issues are in academia, such as PhD students who struggle with depression, sleep-related issues, eating disorders, and suicidal thoughts and behaviors. For example, the article "How to Stay Sane through a PhD: Get Survival Tips from Fellow Students" explains why doctoral students are *sad* and how yoga may serve as a positive activity to "stay grounded amid academic stress" (Weitershausen). This advice is well-intentioned but downplays students' mental health concerns while simultaneously placing the responsibility of mental health on individual students rather than addressing the structures that create and perpetuate an institutional culture of depression, anxiety, and pressure to overcome those feelings. With its reduction of serious mental health issues to mere stress, within a broader series that ignores the institutions that often create and perpetuate these issues, "How to Stay Sane through a PhD" sparked a Twitter conversation about inaccessible academic structures, practices, and attitudes.

Originally begun by graduate student Zara Bain (@zaranosaur), the hashtag #AcademicAbleism was used by a mix of graduate and undergraduate students in the UK and the US to report instances—whether isolated or repeated—of inaccessibility, discrimination, and exclusion in higher education. The majority of the #AcademicAbleism tweets address the challenges students face in trying to secure access to equitable classroom accommodations. There are more than 2,000 tweets that address negotiating and/or securing accommodations through university disability support services and/or talking with instructors. This number does not include the tweets about specific kinds of accommodations, such as captions and subtitles for in-class videos, access to a notetaker, laptop or computer use, extended time on assignments, and adjusted attendance policies. These narratives are written by students with chronic illnesses who drop (or get dropped from) classes because of strict attendance policies, deaf students who are required to watch uncaptioned videos or to read aloud in class, and students whose accommodations are outed because they use laptops in class. Many undergraduate and graduate college students have also used the hashtag to reflect on how their experiences with academic ableism, particularly the lack of institutional accommodations (or instructors who chose not to enact those accommodations), prompted them to leave academia.

The #AcademicAbleism conversation illustrates both the institutional demands for students to overcome their disabilities and also the self-advocacy of students who must overcome inaccessible structures within their university systems. In *The Question of Access: Disability, Space, Meaning,* Tanya Titchkosky writes, "Structures are neither static nor accidental but are, instead, social activities; they carry messages about collective conceptions of people and places, conceptions which themselves come into existence through such social structures and activities" (92). University policies, classroom spaces, and pedagogical practices all carry messages about who belongs in and can access those spaces. Many students do not feel welcome to challenge inaccessible practices with their instructors, and Twitter conversations like #AcademicAbleism, #EverydayAcademicAbleism, and #WhyDisabledPeopleDropOut are channels to voice these experiences, express solidarity, and share strategies with others. As a social space, Twitter invites students, instructors, and administrators to *come over*, identify inaccessible practices, and rewrite more accessible narratives and institutional practices. These conversations highlight the importance of listening to students' needs, because providing accommodations does not require listening to students' *needs* in different contexts; instead, it is a process that listens to *diagnoses*. Twitter is a useful space for coming together to rewrite disability and accessibility narratives, and these conversations can be really useful for providing insight to those of us who work in higher education. However, instructors and administrators also need to create space in programmatic and classroom cultures for listening to students' needs and collaboratively rewriting rhetorics of overcoming.

RHETORICS OF OVERCOMING AND COMING OVER

Writing studies, despite being a relatively new discipline, has established itself as a space to question, analyze, and rewrite narratives about what academic writing should be and who has access (or is denied access) to certain spaces and pedagogical practices. With its attention to access, identity, and different forms of knowing and composing, writing studies is a unique space for counteracting ableist narratives and resisting rhetorics of overcoming. Indeed, there has been critical interdisciplinary work in DS that affects both composition pedagogy and rhetorical studies. In *Disability Rhetoric,* Jay Dolmage explores common disability "myths" or tropes, including overcoming, which requires the individual to surmount their disability through either sheer determination or superhuman strengths:

> In this myth, the person with a disability overcomes their impairment through hard work or has some special talent that offsets their deficiencies. . . . The audience does not have to focus on the disability, or challenge the stigma that this disability entails, but instead refocuses attention toward the "gift." This works as a management of the fears of the temporarily able-bodied (if and when I become disabled, I will compensate or overcome), and it acts as a demand placed upon disabled bodies (you had better be very good at something). (39–40)

Super crips are "courageous or heroic super achievers" (Shapiro 16) who are represented as "'superhuman' because they achieve unexpected accomplishments or live a normal life just like people with no disabilities" (Zhang and Haller 321). Super crips satisfy the desire for overcoming while curtailing fears, but they do not represent all or even the majority of the disabled community. Yet this simultaneous fear of disability and desire for the disabled to overcome is pervasive in different spheres of knowledge production.

In this book, I explore how *rhetorics of overcoming*—discourses promoting the idea that disabled students must overcome their disabilities in order to be successful, to fit in, or to meet the standard—manifest in writing pedagogies through medical-model desires to diagnose students or encourage students to self-disclose and then default to accommodating practices. I identify rhetorics of overcoming as dominant discourses of disability that focus on diagnosis, disclosure, and accommodations. The culture of institutional accommodations in higher education seeks to meet students' needs yet is contingent upon diagnosing and accommodating students on an individual basis. Accommodations are individual measures for individually problemed bodies, and the way institutions often provide them (and instructors receive and interpret them) absolves institutional practices of blame and instead places it on students. Students are responsible for seeking and securing accommodations and, thus, inclusion in academic culture. Accommodations become a way to "fit in" to the mainstream, where "fitting in" rather than challenging oppressive structures is the ultimate goal (Jung 162). Institutional models for accommodations raise an important question: How can we move away from rhetorics of overcoming—the desire to diagnose and accommodate students—to better meet the needs of both disabled and nondisabled students in our classroom and writing center pedagogies?

To be clear, I am not making an argument for the complete eradication of accommodations, but I want to reimagine the current use of accommodations as the only way we meet students' needs—as afterthoughts or retrofits. In *Academic Ableism*, Jay Dolmage writes, "Retrofits like ramps 'fix' space, but retrofits also have a chronicity—a timing and a time logic—that renders them highly temporary yet also relatively unimportant" (70). A student submits accommodation requests every semester. As evidenced by the #AcademicAbleism narratives, this process is not always easy, which sometimes means that students have not secured their accommodations by the time classes start, or that the accommodation is not even applicable—for example, an accommodation granting extra time on tests in a writing class. Retrofitting is not always negative, as it is not always feasible to remove and replace inaccessible structures, but we need to evaluate the process. The sole reliance on accommodations limits the potential to craft more accessible pedagogies, by meeting students' needs *only* if they provide formal documentation.

Throughout this book, I interrogate how rhetorics of overcoming manifest in writing studies scholarship and practices while demonstrating the value of engaging disabled students and instructors in discussions of accessible writing pedagogy—inviting them to *come over* and share their experiences, needs, and expertise. In practice, accessibility is often a unidirectional process, where instructors and administrators only address access within the legal parameters of institutional accommodations and/or try to create accessible physical and digital writing environments without input from disabled students (and instructors) who have valuable experiences that can—and should—inform research practices, curricular development, and pedagogical instruction. I call for development of understandings of disability and difference that move beyond accommodation models in which students are diagnosed and remediated, instead encouraging instructors, administrators, consultants, and students themselves to work together to craft accessible writing pedagogies that meet students' access needs.

I want to imagine a *coming over* narrative that embraces disability, difference, and nonnormative practices—a narrative that informs the crafting of pedagogical practices that welcome a wide range of embodied experiences to *come over* and join the conversation on accessibility. When I first encountered Brenda Brueggemann's multimodal text "Articulating Betweenity: Literacy, Language, Identity, and Technology in the Deaf/Hard-of-Hearing Collection," I was struck by her discussion of *coming over*. She argues that we should not think of students as needing to *overcome*, which suggests a deficit that must be fixed, but rather we need to recognize the importance of students *coming over*, which repositions deficit as "performative gains" (Brueggemann, "Articulating"). Instead of demanding that students overcome language deficiencies, coming over is a commitment to performing what are often deemed as nonnormative expressions of rhetoricity. That is, coming over indicates an embrace—on behalf of both the student and the instructor—of disability and difference. This flips the traditional narrative that positions disability as something that must be overcome in order for student writers to successfully meet literacy and language standards.

Central to this reframing is the concept of "betweenity," a rhetorical process of toggling between decisions and identities and, as often occurs in educational spaces for disabled students, a process of being stuck between experiences and expectations. Brueggemann defines *betweenity* as "a relational space between one's various identities (and others who share, or don't, those identities) and also a relational space constructed by (and through) one's literacy (reading, writing, speaking) skills, particularly in a dominant language." Betweenity can be both an agentive process where disabled students make decisions about how they choose to express and represent themselves, and also a space where student writers get stuck between their own literacy practices and dominant literacy and language standards. In educational environments, betweenity is a space where disabled students are taught dominant literacies, but it also exists as "a space where the deaf other is potentially educating (hearing) others, and younger/distant deaf others as well—often in and through the non-dominant literacies." Betweenity is a back-and-forth process where disabled students negotiate rhetorical and literacy practices with themselves and with instructors, which can be an oppressive space when students are forced to overcome their nonnormative expressions of rhetoricity, but can also be a collaborative space where students share knowledge about literacy and language. It is this tension—between overcoming and coming over—that I explore throughout this book.

To engage in a process of *coming over* necessitates the creation of pedagogical spaces that privilege—not just accommodate—nonnormative literacy practices. And, as I will argue throughout this book, the crafting of multimodal pedagogical spaces makes room for students to perform disability and different literacy practices that acknowledge, respect, and *privilege* a wide range of embodied processes of meaning-making. This privileging not only more wholly enacts socially just and inclusive pedagogies, but also makes room for the composition of more robust, rhetorically rich texts. Importantly, this process of coming over must also invite disabled students to discuss how they best learn and compose, to better facilitate their own learning but also to broaden definitions of literacy and rhetorical expression. This discussion cannot just happen in individual classes once the semester has begun, but must instead take place at the curricular level to prioritize accessibility. I contend that rewriting rhetorics of overcoming as narratives of coming over is one way to overcome ableist pedagogical standards. To come over is to co-construct writing spaces that are accessible and inclusive to students with nonnormative rhetorical practices, presenting students with multiple access points for engaging, learning, and composing. Whereas rhetorics of overcoming rely on medical-model processes of diagnosis, disclosure, cure, and overcoming for individual students, coming over involves the valuing of disability and difference and challenging systemic issues of physical and pedagogical inaccessibility.

COMING OVER IN WRITING STUDIES RESEARCH AND PEDAGOGY

In higher education, there is an expectation for students to learn and demonstrate knowledge in certain ways, and to disclose disabilities in order to have their access needs met if those expectations are inaccessible to them. In writing studies, students are expected to engage dominant literacy practices, engage specific processes and technologies, and compose texts that meet a set of normative criteria. As I will argue throughout *Rhetorics of Overcoming*, these expectations are often ableist and inaccessible to disabled student writers (and more broadly, a wide range of nonnormative student populations), resulting in the need for students to engage in complex processes of disclosure. As noted previously, this toggling between what students *want* and *must* disclose in order to have their access needs met is loaded with power dynamics as students and instructors come together to navigate what access looks like in a writing classroom. I wonder, though: To what extent do students need to disclose disabilities for us to build accessible writing pedagogies? How do we work with each other and with students to develop accessible teaching practices and, by extension, accessible research practices that inform these teaching practices?

Like much cultural rhetorics scholarship, this book reaches across disciplines to develop an accessible framework for disrupting one-size-fits-all pedagogical theories, practices, and methodologies. In particular, I address how attention to DS can inform how we engage disability and accessibility in our research and teaching practices. In "Stories of Methodology: Interviewing Sideways, Crooked and Crip," Margaret Price and Stephanie Kerschbaum note how disability crips[7] the ways in which we imagine, enact, and write about methodology—that is, how centering disability makes visible the exclusionary nature of normative research practices. They claim that "from the beginning, DS scholars have understood that methodology is a key mechanism of disabled peoples' oppression, and that taking back our methodologies is a means of fighting back" (23). Qualitative research is a staple in writing studies research, although there are access issues and normate assumptions about how both researchers and participants should act within the kairotic space of an interview. There is also the issue of how disability is represented within that research.

For this project, I focus on rhetorics of overcoming to interrogate normality and medicalized discourses about disability and writing. As Simi Linton notes, there are many methodological concerns involved with researching disability:

> How does the structure and focus of research contribute to ableist notions of disability? What perspectives inform the choice of variables, theories to be tested, interpretative frameworks to be employed, and subjects/objects to be studied? How has the research agenda been influenced by the absence of disabled people in academic positions? (72–73)

These questions are vital to a study of disability and accessibility, particularly as issues that have either been ignored or not explored thoroughly within writing studies.

Building on the work of disability rhetoricians—such as Dolmage, Kerschbaum, Price, Brueggemann, Vidali, Walters, and Yergeau—who theorize how disability and accessibility have been rhetorically constructed within different contexts, I employ rhetorical analysis to better understand how rhetorics of overcoming have manifested both in writing studies scholarship and in our pedagogical practices. Because attention to disability necessarily means paying close attention to the body, my work is also informed by embodied theories of multimodal and digital composition (Alexander and Rhodes; Arola and Wysocki; Butler, "Embodied Captions" and "Where"; Cedillo; Ceraso, "(Re)Educating" and "Sounding"; Dolmage, "Writing"; Shipka, "Including" and *Toward*; Yergeau et al., "Multimodality"). Building on the methodological work of disability, writing, and multimodality scholars, I developed an institutional review board–approved study in 2014 that involved a survey of undergraduate students enrolled in writing courses across five institutions, a workshop with writing instructors, and follow-up interviews with both students and instructors. Here, I offer snippets from this qualitative research that led me to question the role of disclosures in rhetorics of overcoming, reflecting on the methodological challenges of developing an ethical qualitative study of accessibility and negotiating disability disclosures—both students' and my own.

Inviting Students to Come Over and Share Their Experiences with (In)Accessibility

I frequently encounter arguments from other instructors and administrators that disabled students' needs are *dramatically* different from those of nondisabled students, that their learning needs are beyond what we can adequately prepare for in the space of a writing classroom, or even that we must make decisions about what is best for disabled students because they cannot articulate their own needs. To design more accessible writing pedagogies, we must value and listen to the needs articulated by all students—those who disclose disabilities and those who do not. Specifically, I argue that we need to cultivate spaces for students to share these needs in ways that are not othering. To better understand the dynamics of accessibility and how students understand their needs in writing classrooms, I surveyed undergraduate students about their experiences in college writing classes, from specific questions about disability and accommodations to broader questions about the use of multimodality in their writing classes.

This study was fraught with disclosure negotiations, from drafting questions to conducting follow-up interviews with participants: *Do I ask students to disclose disabilities? Do I disclose disabilities?* For the survey, I asked students whether they identified as disabled but chose not to require them to disclose those disabilities. Instead, after asking whether students identified as disabled, I asked, "If yes, is this an important part of how you perceive yourself as a writer (how you read, learn, understand texts, brainstorm ideas, write and revise)?" Seven of 121 students disclosed disabilities, and five indicated that their identification with disability was an important part of how they perceived themselves as writers and secured accommodations. There were three students who indicated that they did not identify as disabled but had requested and received accommodations, which legally requires a disability diagnosis and documentation process. These results left me wondering about self-identification and how to create systems of support that aren't reliant on disability disclosures and diagnoses.

My questions about the role and ethics of disclosure in the classroom and research contexts intensified during a follow-up interview with a creative writing major, Tiana.[8] She disclosed an issue with multiple stimuli in her survey, and an hour into our interview about disability identity, disclosures, and rhetorics of overcoming, Tiana offered another disclosure: "Throughout my life, I've dealt on and off with these issues of depression and anxiety. I mentioned this multiple stimuli thing that I have, so I can't deal with multiple stimuli. So these are ways that make my brain if not disabled [then] unique, you know what I mean?" She had not disclosed depression or anxiety in the survey, and I was interested in why she had mentioned it. What had changed in our conversation that Tiana felt comfortable disclosing that information, and what did she gain from it?

Disability disclosures are never static: they are contextual to situations and to audiences. In "On Rhetorical Agency and Disclosing Disability in Academic Writing," Kerschbaum draws on Price's notion of *kairotic* spaces, "the less formal, often unnoticed, areas of academe where knowledge is produced and power is exchanged" (Price, *Mad at School* 60), to argue that disability disclosures exist within complex systems of "circulating narratives of disability and able-bodiedness, relationships among interlocutors, and institutional and environmental contexts" (Kerschbaum, "On Rhetorical Agency" 63). People make sense of different discourses in relation to their own experiences and goals for how they want to identify themselves and be identified by others, and students often engage in a process of "risk management" (Wood, "Rhetorical") when making choices about when and where to disclose. There are many reasons why a student may not disclose, and in the kairotic space of our interview, I had not thought of creating a space where we could exchange knowledge; rather, I had established a space where Tiana would share knowledge with me and where I held the power, as someone conducting disability research without disclosing my own position with regard to disability, which may have reinforced my able-bodied appearance.

Prompted by Tiana's disclosure, I decided to disclose my own history with and scholarly interests in disability and writing. I wasn't sure what to expect from that disclosure—whether Tiana would address it, build from it, or simply ignore it—but she immediately responded by explaining her interconnected experiences with depression, anxiety, and writing:

> When I was a teenager . . . I had issues with depression, anxiety, and I was seeing counselors, and those are *problems* that have never gone away for me. Especially when I was in college for a while it just got really bad. I was still doing [*pause*] you know my work in the classroom, I was getting really good grades, and I was involved in a lot of things. And for all intents and purposes, I was a functional human being except for the fact that I was completely overridden by these feelings, which I think more people have than admit to them. I learned slowly throughout college, the more I wrote then the better I felt.

She explained that what caused her anxiety was something that she could harness to compose detailed, thoughtful writing. Throughout the interview, Tiana positioned herself as someone whose needs were not frequently met in writing classes and who disclosed disabilities but did not receive accommodations. In an academic culture where we meet students' needs based largely on diagnoses and formal accommodations, where does that leave students like Tiana?

Inviting Instructors to Come Over to Discussions of Accessibility

In addition to learning from students, I wanted to create space for writing instructors and consultants to share concerns and strategies about accessible classroom practices. I organized a workshop for writing faculty and graduate students to introduce universal design (UD) and multimodality as frameworks for identifying inaccessible classroom structures and to brainstorm inclusive practices; I then conducted follow-up interviews with instructors. To preface this conversation, I shared the survey results that I had collected in order to foreground students' experiences *before* discussing how to craft more accessible and inclusive practices. Three key themes emerged from this workshop: how to accommodate what we don't know or can't see, how to develop accessible practices at both the classroom and curricular levels, and how to accommodate students whose accommodations don't apply to writing classes.

A common refrain in the instructor workshop was that it is easy to determine the accessibility of physical environments but more difficult to determine pedagogical inaccessibility. During an interview, I asked one of the instructors, Brian, to articulate his understanding of accessibility:

> I think of [accessibility] as providing a range of opportunities [for students] to do the work of the course or follow their own desires or come up with their objectives or values but in a range of different ways. So I'm thinking of it as access points. Access points that some students are going to be able to reach more easily based on maybe ability, but then having enough of those so that students can feel like based on their individual ability and whether it has to do with overcoming a particular type of mental or physical handicap or not—or what they conceive of as a handicap or what has been diagnosed as one.

Talking openly with students about how assignments may benefit particular types of learners and creating access points where students can engage with content differently are small-scale practices that can help cultivate a culture of accessibility. On a larger scale, discussing accessibility in composition pedagogy classes and teacher training seminars instills an awareness of the many different ways students learn and make meaning. Foregrounding accessibility means evaluating how we—as practitioners, as scholars—value and engage with difference.

One faculty member, Elijah, disclosed a learning disability during our interview, connecting his understandings of accessibility to his experiences as a writing center administrator with a learning disability. As I discuss in Chapter 3, writing center discourses of accessibility and disability are often framed in terms of diagnosis and accommodation, as Elijah acknowledged: "If we can see a student or some aspect of a student that indicates some form or level of disability, because it's obvious and because it's harder to ignore, that oftentimes becomes a focus both in literature and also how [writing center staff]—whether it's instructors or tutors—approach their work." This resonates with a diagnose-and-accommodate approach to disability, but, because of his own invisible disability, Elijah noted that he tried to be mindful of the unknowns:

> I only am aware of the things that students are willing to disclose, so part of that for me is being open [about] my own learning disability, trying to get students to feel comfortable to be willing to disclose information so that I can hopefully rethink my classroom or rethink my tutoring strategies and approaches in a way that's going to help those students.

Self-disclosures are rhetorical strategies that are shaped by embodied experiences and are dependent on context. Elijah reflected on his own experiences and self-disclosed in the kairotic space of the one-on-one consulting session to make students feel comfortable sharing their own learning needs. This is not unlike my disclosure to Tiana, which created space for a dialogue.

A METHODOLOGY FOR RESISTING RHETORICS OF OVERCOMING

I opened this chapter with a few disclosures of my own, which in many ways is an ethical necessity for folks engaging in disability work—something I discuss later in this section. It is my goal to frame disclosure as a form of rhetoricity; that is, disclosure can function strategically to build writing environments that more fully account for a wide range of students' and instructors' needs. Disclosure was a dominant theme throughout both the students' and the instructors' responses about disability and accessibility that I highlighted in the previous section. Although the study was limited in scope, what I learned from creating space to listen to the needs of disabled and nondisabled writing students was the significance of (self-)disclosure in the process of ensuring pedagogical accessibility. Ultimately, this research raised questions for me about the ethics of disclosure in both research and pedagogical contexts:

- What are the rhetorical potentials and risks of researchers disclosing to participants in studies of accessibility and disability?
- What are the rhetorical potentials of students disclosing disabilities to their instructors and classmates? In contrast, how do external demands for disclosure harm students' learning? What risks do students face when they disclose in face-to-face, digital, and anonymous environments?
- How do we create pedagogical spaces that do not rely solely on systems of diagnosis and disclosure to ensure accessibility for disabled student writers?

These are questions that I hope to address throughout *Rhetorics of Overcoming*. And although there are no easy answers to any of these questions, I rely on DS theory and methodology as frameworks for better understanding these issues and designing more inclusive research and pedagogical practices.

Disability studies methodology draws attention to whose voices and narratives are represented in our research and how we ethically and inclusively represent ourselves and our participants in our research. In "Disability Studies Methodology: Explaining Ourselves to Ourselves," Margaret Price observes that "like DS scholarship more generally, DS methodology aims at a radical reshaping of relations of power" (164) in terms of whose knowledges and experiences are valued and represented—and why. Price draws on Mary Louise Pratt's discussion of contact zones to identify four contact zones that shape DS methodology: access, activism, identification, and representation. DS methodology builds on feminist and social justice methodologies by encouraging researchers to be critical of long-held methods that may be inaccessible to researchers and/or participants, to adapt our methods, and to be reflexive and transparent about our practices. Being reflexive about how we represent ourselves and our participants means we must always be ready to adapt to the kairotic situation of the qualitative interview, so the disability researcher is not wholly participant nor observer, objective nor subjective (Brueggemann, "Still-Life" 19–20). Rather, we toggle between these roles. This state of betweenity emphasizes the complexities of the power dynamics in disability research: disability is dynamic, and accessibility must always be negotiated.

Taking up DS research involves questioning who we imagine as our participants when we design studies, and making space for our own identifications with disability. Price writes, "I argue that DS research must make more space for explicit identification by researchers—not in a rote, 'here's my diagnosis' way, but in ways that are characterized by creativity, contradiction, and revision over time" ("Disability" 169). When I first presented data from this study in 2015, an audience member raised their hand and told me that I read as nondisabled. And for the purposes of the survey that I distributed, I did not disclose otherwise. Brueggemann warns that self-reflexivity "risks turning representation into a solipsistic, rhetorical position in which the researcher (the self)—ah, once again—usurps the position of the subject (the other). For in being self-reflexive, we turn the lens back on ourselves, put ourselves at the center of representation" ("Still-Life" 19). I didn't want to fixate on myself, yet found myself disclosing in follow-up interviews to build connections. In *Toward a New Rhetoric of Difference*, Kerschbaum describes resisting disclosure because she was not studying herself: "But that sense of detachment was the very thing—or one of the main things—that kept me from really understanding that my experience of deafness was not just something that happened to me, but also something that others took up in various and complicated ways" (24). Disclosure and self-reflexivity can be channels for more deeply engaging research, particularly studies of disability and accessibility.

To actively resist rhetorics of overcoming, it is of theoretical and political importance for disability researchers to state their subject positions in complex and meaningful ways, because "stating that one identifies as disabled or nondisabled calls attention to the absent voice of disabled people in scholarship and illustrates that the reader may tend to make the assumption, although probably not consciously, that the writer is nondisabled" (Linton 153). In the context of the researcher-participant relationship, not sharing my positionality with participants—coupled with a lack of visible disabilities—may have read not as an attempt at objectivity but as a performance of able-bodiedness. Disclosing is an opportunity to build trust, and disclosures can and should move beyond a disabled/nondisabled binary to include familial, work, social, and political relationships to disability (Corbett). Disability studies offers a way to think about disclosure differently: rather than being used as a mechanism to formulate prescribed practices that are designed to address the checklist characteristics of a diagnosed disability, disclosure can be used rhetorically to build accessible support systems.

Although I will illustrate the ways in which disclosure can be stigmatizing and harmful, I also hope to illustrate the ways in which students, tutors, instructors, and administrators can use disclosure rhetorically. Disclosures can be used to build community and to share access needs, and they operate as tangible reminders of the material needs of students. As I turn toward UD and multimodality as two theoretical frameworks that writing instructors and administrators can use to resist rhetorics of overcoming, disclosure serves as an important reminder to center students' embodied experiences and needs when designing pedagogical infrastructures.

CHAPTER BREAKDOWN

I begin Chapter 2 ("(De)Valuing Disability: Moving beyond Accommodation Approaches to Accessibility in Writing Studies") by contextualizing and historicizing overcoming within the field of writing studies, highlighting the dominant discourses that have influenced our pedagogical theories about disability and writing. I focus first on scholarship that aligns with medical and social models of disability, arguing that we can better understand the field's treatment of nonnormative student writers by placing medical-model and basic writing discourses in conversation. Then I address how social models of disability have been applied to writing studies, exploring UD and multimodality as two theories that can inform an embodied multimodal writing pedagogy and move *beyond* the accommodation approach that informs prevailing scholarship, practices, and attitudes for and toward disability.

Multimodal composing and teaching practices are widespread, and theories that highlight the multiple and diverse ways that students know, learn, and compose can help instructors and administrators proactively construct accessible pedagogical environments rather than defaulting to accommodation. In addition to writing classrooms, I explore accommodation approaches to accessibility in writing center contexts in Chapter 3 ("Resisting Diagnosis and Creating Avenues for Agency in the Writing Center"), identifying the ways in which rhetorics of overcoming have influenced writing center scholarship and pedagogy in order to theorize accessible consulting practices grounded in theories of UD and multimodality. I argue that the rhetorical agency built into multimodal pedagogies offers students, consultants, and instructors flexibility in finding access points and negotiating their learning and composing needs without moving through a process of diagnosis, accommodation, and overcoming. In Chapter 4, "Guaranteeing Access(ibility) in the Multimodal Writing Classroom," I offer a framework that foregrounds accessibility as an integral part of rhetorical practice, highlighting accessible multimodal practices that instructors can adapt for their writing classrooms.

Finally, I conclude in Chapter 5 ("Toward an Ethics of Accessibility") with snapshots of how rhetorics of overcoming shape my day-to-day experiences of navigating campus. I do so to illustrate how these narratives of overcoming are both reinforced and resisted in different contexts. Specifically, I illustrate how multimodality and UD manifest in ways that increase accessibility and work toward disability justice in university settings, and how—in other ways—inaccessible spaces could benefit from a universally designed, multimodal lens. Ultimately, I contend that explicitly addressing disability and accessibility in conversations about literacy and writing in multiple modes is necessary for foregrounding the role of accessibility in composing.

Increasingly, a range of students' abilities, disabilities, technological literacies, and comfort levels are present in the classroom, and it is simply not reasonable to think that students can or should always access all modes equally well. Indeed, during our interview, Tiana asked, "Disability is just sort of about mode of learning and alternative modes of learning, and how do you get away from a structure that doesn't actually apply to a large percentage of kids because they're learning and receiving information in different ways?" There is a complex landscape of needs in the college writing classroom—particularly in first-year writing—and many of these needs are never disclosed. Writing instructors and administrators need to redesign pedagogical structures that necessitate a disability disclosure or diagnosis and reinforce rhetorics of overcoming, developing practices that instead foreground accessibility and reaffirm students' embodied ways of learning and composing. In the following chapters, I illustrate how theories of UD and multimodal composition can increase the accessibility of writing pedagogy, but this process involves *coming over* to a different orientation to disability and accessibility—one that requires listening to the needs of students and valuing the experiences, knowledges, and literacies they bring into the classroom.

2

(De)Valuing Disability: Moving beyond Accommodation Approaches to Accessibility in Writing Studies

> Disability has a troubled history in college composition. For most of the twentieth century, people with disabilities were institutionalized in asylums, "schools" for the "feeble-minded," and other exclusionary institutions: locations deemed the inverse of the college or university. The ethic of higher education encourages students and teachers alike to accentuate ability, valorize perfection, and stigmatize anything that hints at intellectual (or physical) weakness.
> —Jay Dolmage et al., "'I Simply Gave Up Trying to Present at CCCC...'"

AT A FACULTY SENATE MEETING, a hand was raised: "Do we have to accommodate that?" Someone had voiced a concern about the increasing number of accommodation letters that granted students absences beyond those designated in the professor's attendance policy, and another questioned whether such requests were crossing a line.

Strict attendance policies can become one more barrier that students with mental and psychiatric disabilities, chronic illnesses, and autoimmune disorders must overcome. We had many discussions that semester about the increasing number of students disclosing mental health crises, and these new accommodations were met with suspicion and perceived as degrading the integrity of instructors' classes—classes that students couldn't afford to miss. Faculty wanted to help students with mental disabilities, but not at the expense of granting accommodations that they deemed unnecessary. Accessibility is a concept that is easy to applaud but is not so easy to enact without reinforcing hierarchies of exclusion, wherein some bodies and minds are deemed less worthy than others. Following the Americans with Disabilities Act (ADA) language of *reasonable accommodations*, instructors are willing to help, but only *within reason*. Providing extra time on a test is considered reasonable because it only requires that faculty refer students to a campus testing lab, but redesigning the course to eliminate timed tests—or in this example, eliminating attendance policies—moves beyond the realm of reason.

Disability has had a troubled history in higher education and within writing studies; however, there have been bursts of attention to disability and accessibility in writing studies scholarship that reflect different cultural understandings and recurring discourses that have circulated about overcoming disability—and, by extension, nonnormative student populations. Disability studies has also received some significant attention in writing studies, to the point where it was once considered "new. Different. Hot" (Price, "Accessing" 53). Despite this, disability still functions as an absent presence. Disabled students are present in college writing classes and writing centers, yet their voices go unheard. Disability is increasingly discussed and theorized in academic research, yet disability and accessibility are often absent from curricular and pedagogical considerations. As noted previously, instructors may not think of disability until presented with an accommodations letter that makes visible both disability and the inaccessible practices of that class structure.

The purpose of this chapter is to outline and highlight connections between some of the dominant discourses that have influenced writing studies scholarship, disciplinary understandings and attitudes about disabled student writers, and pedagogical practices. First, I highlight how rhetorics of overcoming disability emerged within basic writing discourses of nonnormative student populations that approached disability from a medical diagnosis model.[9] Then I address accommodation approaches to accessibility that recognize structural issues but are marked by neoliberal values of efficiency and individualism, treating disability as an individual issue that must be individually solved, and failing to acknowledge inaccessible infrastructures. I explore multimodal composition and DS—specifically, universal design—as two pedagogical frameworks that can be adopted to resist rhetorics of overcoming. Specifically, I argue that multimodal and UD writing pedagogies make visible inaccessible practices, move beyond normative conceptions of writing, and act as productive sites of *coming over* by encouraging students to be part of the conversation about accessibility. Instructors and administrators cannot exclusively be the decision-makers about accessibility, without allowing students to share their learning and composing needs. It is tempting to imagine this as a linear movement away from rhetorics of overcoming and toward an acceptance of different composing processes, yet normative values and medical-model orientations are often entangled within these discourses. I conclude this chapter by sharing student examples in order to highlight some of the composing strategies that are enabled by disabled embodiments. Ultimately, I hope to illustrate how multimodal pedagogies that attend to both embodiment and UD offer a way to ensure accessibility that is rooted neither in diagnosis nor in universalized terms.

Assessing the affordances and constraints of different pedagogical approaches to disability and disabled student writers helps to contextualize how rhetorics of overcoming have manifested in scholarship and practices, reinforcing desires for standard writing produced by standard bodies. Of course, these desires for normalcy and negative perceptions about people who do not act or speak or write in normative ways are deeply ingrained in everyday and academic cultures. Paying attention to the disciplinary discourses that ebb and flow as cultural understandings of disability and pedagogy shift illuminates the complexities of the field's treatment and (de)valuing of disabled student writers, providing insight to chart more accessible, inclusive paths for future scholarship and practices.

DIAGNOSING AND REMEDIATING THE DISABLED STUDENT WRITER

At different moments, disability has been loosely defined within contexts of deficit, which DS scholars have illustrated through the continued segregation of students of color and disabled students in specialized classes (Connor and Ferri; Erevelles et al.; Ferri). Labels for "deficient" students have included "ineducable, handicapped, culturally and linguistically deprived, semilingual, and, more recently, at-risk" (Crawford and Bartolomé 160). Ideologies of disability as deficit continue to influence how we categorize and label certain groups of people as deviant, even in postsecondary contexts. For example, Mina Shaughnessy acknowledges the slippery language of disability deficit when addressing ethnically and racially diverse students, and makes an effort in *Errors and Expectations: A Guide for the Teacher of Basic Writing* "to demonstrate how the sources of [basic writers'] difficulties can be explained without recourse to such pedagogically empty terms as 'handicapped' or 'disadvantaged'" (4). In this section, I trace how rhetorics of overcoming emerged through basic writing discourses of disability as a deficit to be diagnosed and remediated. The overlapping discourses of diagnosing disabled student writers and remediating basic writers offer insight into the historical treatment of nonnormative student writers.

There is a history of the college writing classroom as a remedial space for many marginalized student populations. Indeed, the Committee on Disability Issues in College Composition describes the composition classroom as "the place to temporarily store, fix, and cure students deemed unready for college. College is both a landing and launching space for the 'most able.' But the composition classroom has always been located slightly off this runway" (Dolmage et al. 57). Acknowledging disciplinary discourses that position disabled students as similar to basic writers can help instructors and administrators make sense of how these associations, labels, and remediative discourses influence our desires to diagnose and remediate disability. In the context of writing classrooms, a medical model of disability positions students as individuals who must be fixed or cured of their deficits—that is, they must overcome them. This manifests in scholarship wherein disability is something that instructors must cope with and that, often, cannot be helped through standard pedagogical practices and instead must be remediated. Remediation models have been contested both in writing studies scholarship (Barber-Fendley and Hamel; Brueggemann et al.; Hull and Rose; Rose; White) and in writing center scholarship (Grimm, "Rearticulating"; Harris; North). However, as Amy Vidali has argued, there are strong parallels between the disabled writer and basic writer, and they have been positioned similarly in early writing studies discussions of disability, which are reflective of cultural understandings of disability and basic writers that were dominant in the late 1970s and 1980s.

Deficit-oriented discourse necessitates overcoming in order for the disabled student to be successful, to fit in, or to meet the standard. Although there is nothing wrong with someone working hard, "it is the expectation or demand that a person with a disability 'overcome' their 'tragic' state that disability studies scholars find problematic" (Vidali 46). Within writing studies, this discourse manifests in different ways but is perhaps most recognizable in the context of the basic writer. In "Discourses of Disability and Basic Writing," Vidali explores how deficit has manifested both in basic writing's roots in cognitivism and in medical models of disability. Vidali writes, "While basic writing scholars situate such deficit theories as debunked approaches of the past, disability studies scholars emphasize that deficit theories dominate the perception of disability in the present" (42). The similarities in how basic writers and disabled students have been perceived as flawed and have received remedial treatment illuminate the pervasiveness of the medical model in basic writing discourse. Both groups of students are also positioned within overcoming narratives that highlight their deficits as individual issues. For basic writers, the expectation to overcome places the responsibility on the student and erases institutional, disciplinary, and programmatic responsibility and accountability. By acknowledging these connections and the ways that "a particular set of students might be labeled 'basic' at one historical or institutional moment and 'disabled' the next" (44), we gain fuller understandings of the pervasiveness of deficit discourse that still manifests within our pedagogical practices.

An example of this deficit-oriented approach to disability is learning disability (LD) scholarship focused on diagnosis and remediation, which emerged in the 1980s. For example, Amy Richards published an article in the *Journal of Basic Writing* wherein she states that the "chief hope for the writing disabled student in the college classroom is that English composition instructors learn how to make tentative identification of writing dysfunction" so that they may be tested, diagnosed, or at least recognized "not as mentally retarded, emotionally impaired, or grossly illiterate but as students having a disability that prevents them from processing language adequately, a disability that does not yield to usual remediative techniques" (68). An LD diagnosis separates students from arguably worse labels that they cannot overcome, yet this diagnosis "both predict[s] and determine[s] outcomes by denying or providing medical treatments or educational services" (Wilson and Lewiecki-Wilson 11). Disability studies scholars have shown that LD students are frequently undervalued in educational settings when they fail to conform to an overcoming narrative of adopting a positive attitude and working hard to overcome their deficit.

Many other composition articles have served as guides to understanding learning disabilities by defining LD, detailing characteristics that manifest within specific writing behaviors, and offering teaching strategies for working with LD students.[10] Rhetorics of overcoming undergird these articles through the emphasis on individual deficits and checklist-style characteristics that instructors can use to diagnose and work with LD students—characteristics that can be overcome and checked off one at a time. The idea that students want to be diagnosed so that they can access appropriate support services contains a certain element of truth: disabled students want pedagogical support. But do students need to be diagnosed to access support? What is communicated about disability and disabled students when access is framed in terms of pathology and remediation? What positive contributions, skills, and composing insights get lost in such framings?

ACCOMMODATING THE DISABLED STUDENT WRITER

Generally, writing instructors and scholars have moved beyond remediation and the idea that disabled students are beyond the help of instructor expertise, yet remnants of medical-model discourses surface through a focus on individual accommodations in response to medically categorized characteristics of a specific disability diagnosis. An accommodation approach to disability is shaped by the institutional system of disability accommodations—a service designed to meet the pedagogical needs of disabled college students. This system relies on formal diagnosis and a semester-by-semester negotiation with administration and faculty of the appropriate accommodations for each course, and it addresses accessibility at the individual level.

Accommodation approaches to disability are often informed by disability rights discourses of advocacy, yet position disability as an impairment that is specific to individual students, who are responsible for overcoming those differences. This impairment-specific approach focuses on diagnostic categories and "may limit students and teachers to consider specific disabilities and specific solutions instead of encouraging more comprehensive understandings of disability and ability as contingent bodily states affected by time, space, and a range of fluid contexts" (Walters 429). Walters articulates a pedagogical approach that reacts against the valuing of diagnosis and corresponding static practices—an approach that rejects the idea that individual, "reasonable" accommodations are the only solution to meet students' needs. Though impairment-specific models of accessibility have a place in higher education to account for and accommodate the material experiences of disabled students in the classroom, this approach ignores more critical discussions and understandings of disability and, thus, accessibility. Discourses of accommodation draw from social constructions of disability and creation of accessible learning environments, but still hold many of the deep-rooted medicalized attitudes and assumptions about disability. They represent a well-intentioned approach that seeks to meet students' needs yet still positions disability as something *different*.

Often, university-sanctioned accommodations are positioned as the standard means of support for students who identify as disabled. Accommodations position students as subjects who must be diagnosed and then cured of their deficits in order to succeed within our classrooms. Linda Feldmeier White argues that understanding disability as an individualized issue allows education systems to frame disability as an unexpected failure that does not require systemic change (726). The student is responsible for seeking and securing the accommodation and, thus, inclusion into academic culture, which positions accommodations as a way to "fit in" to the mainstream, where "fitting in" rather than challenging oppressive structures is the ultimate goal (Jung 162). While accommodations are important for providing students with academic support, the accommodation process emphasizes disability as something that is largely the responsibility of the student.

Even if a student successfully acquires accommodations, those accommodations rarely apply to writing classes because they focus on assessments such as testing, do not account for students' specific material needs, and do not explicitly support the work promoted within composition classrooms (Barber-Fendley and Hamel 528–29). In his discussion of accommodation transfer, Neil Simpkins draws attention to the extra layer of labor for writing students whose accommodations aren't applicable to writing contexts: "Even with the guidance of disability services, it takes experimentation and time to know what type and degree of modification one needs to write." That is, providing students with opportunities to create their accommodations, while seemingly facilitating accessibility, may create additional barriers for students to overcome. Accommodation discourses present disability as something that goes away once accommodated, so there is little space to negotiate accommodations after they have been granted. Dolmage describes this as a lack of a feedback loop: "If an accommodation is given, the student is expected to be thankful and happy, regardless of the fit of the accommodation or its efficacy" (*Academic* 81). Of course, there are some universities where students are given the agency to choose their accommodations, which in theory could replace the need for a feedback loop, yet this places further responsibility on individual students. Within the institutional structures and constraints of higher education, accommodations help writing instructors legally support students, but what do we communicate about valuing accessibility and inclusivity when we rely on bare-minimum approaches to accessibility?

The current model for accommodations raises many questions about meeting students' needs: *How can we meet the needs of all students without relying solely on accommodations for some? How do we resist the desire for accommodations to be enough to help students overcome their disabilities?* Asking questions about our individual, programmatic, and institutional attitudes about accommodations and disability is a necessary first step in assessing how to build accessible structures moving forward. White argues that integrating disability into our pedagogical considerations—in crafting assignments and assessments—can allow us to examine "whether teaching practices that require accommodations are really necessary" (728). Rather than accommodating individual students who cannot succeed within classroom environments that limit their means of engaging and composing, instructors need to assess and overcome inaccessible writing pedagogies.

Accommodation approaches seek to meet students' needs by acknowledging and removing barriers to equitable access in classroom environments, but they require diagnosis and do not require structural redesign—just temporary changes. Accommodations are deemed appropriate by disability service organizations and mediated by instructors, and students are often removed from the process, which results in accommodations that are made based on diagnostic criteria alone and not material experiences. Ultimately, they do not fully allow disabled students' abilities to be recognized or invoked. Instead of relying on retrofitting our teaching practices through accommodations, we need to prioritize accessibility in the design of classroom spaces and practices. What I want to suggest is something more radical than accommodations: a version of accessibility that is rooted in students' material experiences, that is collaborative and reflective—accessibility driven by social justice and student agency rather than accessibility driven by obligation.

MAKING SPACE FOR DISABLED AND NONNORMATIVE COMPOSING PRACTICES

Disability studies can inform how writing instructors and administrators engage with embodied and nonnormative processes of composing in writing environments. DS rejects and reacts against rhetorics of overcoming that position students as responsible for overcoming their disabilities in order to access equitable treatment. Writing studies scholars have taken up DS to resist pathologization of disability and different composing processes. "Becoming Visible: Lessons in Disability," published in *College Composition and Communication* in 2001, shows the ways in which DS is important to writing studies as a field with a deep-rooted history of making marginalized bodies and voices visible, and contends that writing instructors are rhetorically equipped to do this by challenging deficit-oriented language and constructions of "normal" and "abnormal" ways of learning, being, and writing (Brueggemann et al. 370). For example, Patricia Dunn advocates for integrating multimodal, collaborative writing instruction to deconstruct our notions of normal writing, arguing, "When we expect all students—and ourselves—to think in oral, visual, and kinesthetic arenas, in addition to the ones that privilege written words, we learn from those who were previously excluded" (381).[11] Multimodal practices are opportunities for writing instructors to make disability visible by encouraging embodied composing processes and offering students multiple access points to engage course content, rather than relying on a specific modality that is inaccessible and thus positions disabled composing processes as problems to be overcome.

Disability studies shares and enhances many of the core values of writing studies, with additional attention to disability as a valuable asset to the learning and composing process, a critical modality, and a rhetorical way of being. The questions raised by DS "ask us to think carefully about language and its effects, to understand the role of the body in learning and writing, to view bodies and minds as inherently and wonderfully divergent, to consider issues of access and exclusion in policies and in the environment, and to reengage with theories of difference and diversity" (Lewiecki-

Wilson and Brueggemann 1). In this section, I discuss how theories of multimodality and UD can be valuable frameworks for better understanding the value of disabled composing processes and rhetorical expression, and for rewriting overcoming narratives about disabled student writers. Specifically, I argue that multimodal, universally designed writing pedagogies make visible inaccessible practices, move beyond normative conceptions of writing, and act as productive sites of *coming over* by encouraging students to be part of the conversation about accessibility. I advocate for writing pedagogies informed by both UD and multimodality because multimodal writing pedagogies are often still entangled in normative values. Multimodal practices linked to UD have potential to model a collective and complex accessible environment, and this framework can offer us ways to make institutions multimodal in how they engage with students in a post-diagnosis-and-accommodation landscape.

Multimodal Composition and the Nonnormative Composing Body

It has become a truism in writing studies that writing classes teach students rhetorical and metacommunicative awareness—not simply technical *skills*. Rhetorical awareness develops throughout the writing process as students make choices about what to research, set goals for their projects, and decide what media are most appropriate for their message, audience, and context. In *Toward a Composition Made Whole*, Jody Shipka argues for a multimodal framework that "requires students to assume responsibility for determining the purposes, potentials, and contexts of their work" (88). This framework grants flexibility in the range of materials and technologies that students can use, which can increase accessibility and challenges students to make their own rhetorical choices about the process and production of their texts. A multimodal framework values a nuanced rhetorical awareness of both argument and medium. Specifically, Shipka contends that instead of focusing on genres that students can reproduce, "what is crucial is that students leave their courses exhibiting a more nuanced awareness of the various choices they make, or even fail to make, throughout the process of producing a text and . . . carefully consider the effect those choices might have on others" (85). Providing students with multiple access points, modes, and media to engage and produce content is necessary for developing students' rhetorical awareness in ways that are accessible.

A shared goal of multimodality and UD is multiplicity in teaching, learning, and composing practices. For example, multimodal teaching practices acknowledge that students benefit from information presented in different ways, brief lectures accompanied by slides or videos, collaborative work, large-class discussions or paired discussions, and interactive workshops. Multimodal pedagogies promote the use of any number of media to create cohesive rhetorical texts, allowing students different modes of communication to compose and produce knowledge. For example, a multimodal research project could take the form of a podcast with primary and secondary research, an infographic that combines data and storytelling, a hand-printed and bound zine that synthesizes different perspectives, or a poster presentation. Creating learning environments with multiple ways for students to engage and compose can increase accessibility for disabled student writers—even those who do not disclose—by giving them agency for rhetorical expression and providing multiple access points, instead of presenting one option for composing that may be inaccessible to students, who must then overcome this pedagogical barrier in order to succeed.

Still, I want to make clear that there is nothing inherently accessible or anti-ableist about multimodal writing pedagogies. Although I believe that multimodality has the potential to be an accessible pedagogical framework, it has been normalized by narrow conceptions of rhetoric and composition. Multimodal composing is often assumed to be inclusive and accessible because of its valuing of alternative modes of communication, and it can be, but is often undergirded with ableist assumptions about the person composing the text and people engaging with the text. For example, imagining multimodality as translating one mode (text) to another mode (audio) is a limiting way to imagine the rhetorical potential of multimodal texts and is limiting to students who cannot access the assignment because there is only one mode of expression. Another common writing assignment is scripting and producing a podcast, which may not account for a deaf student or deaf audience by requiring a written transcript. The same is true for the increasing number of rhetoric and writing studies podcasts that offer a wealth of knowledge from scholars and activists and teachers in the field, which could be great disciplinary and pedagogical resources if made accessible.

Adopting different technologies in the classroom can call attention to normative conceptions of embodiment and writing. Disciplinary attention to digital media has prompted attention to technologies that privilege or exclude certain bodies (Butler, "Embodied Captions" and "Where"; Meyer; Yergeau et al., "Multimodality"; Zdenek, "Accessible Podcasting," *Reading*, and "Which"). In "Writing against Normal: Navigating a Corporeal Turn," Dolmage advocates for development of technologies and pedagogies that affirm bodies and examine "the messy and recursive process of composing" rather than looking at "ideal, complete texts" that mirror ideal, normative bodies (125). He presents wikis as an example of a technology that *disables* the linear composing process and presents a different way for students to navigate a composing environment, moving back and forth through different versions and writing with different people. Everyday technologies like speech-to-text software on smartphones and computers, text-to-speech features in Microsoft Word and Google Docs, and asynchronous communication platforms encourage and facilitate nonnormative forms of expression. Incorporating accessible technologies in writing classes minimizes formal processes that single out and accommodate individuals, and instead encourages all students to use resources that facilitate their composing processes.

Multimodal pedagogies that encourage the use of technology to compose and learn can create opportunities for students who do not engage with normative teaching and composing practices, but digital-only approaches to multimodality can also create extra barriers that students must overcome. The term *multimodal* is often conflated with *digital*, but designing and enacting multimodal pedagogies does not necessitate the use of digital tools and media. Jody Shipka has argued throughout her multimodal scholarship that we should not limit students' materials for composing:

> If we are committed to creating courses that provide students with opportunities to forge new connections, to work in highly flexible ways, and to become increasingly cognizant of the ways texts provide shape for and take shape from the contexts in which they are produced, circulated, valued, and responded to, it is crucial . . . that we not limit the range of materials or technologies students might take up and alter in compelling ways. ("Including" 84)

Providing students with the option to choose between physical and digital modes to achieve specific learning goals and outcomes is more accessible than limiting them to digital media or even to a single mode—unless, of course, that is an essential outcome of the assignment or course.[12] Expanding multimodality beyond the digital makes space for students to draw on a range of embodied literacies.

The communicative actions and potentials of our bodies—our embodied being—cannot exist outside of our specific cultural contexts or the technologies that we use to consume and produce texts (Wysocki 8). Media are embodied, but there are specific embodiments that produce specific kinds of writing that are privileged in college writing classrooms. In *On Multimodality: New Media in Composition Studies,* Jonathan Alexander and Jacqueline Rhodes discuss how incorporating multimodality into writing classrooms can help instructors teach "the many ways in which the consumption and production of multimedia texts impacts how we conceive and understand contemporary subjectivity" (175). Indeed, I argue that multimodal pedagogies can give students space to embody disability and resist mainstream discourses about disability (Hitt). To incorporate multimodality into the writing classroom, instructors must pay critical attention both to the interplays between media and subjectivity and to the forms of embodiment that writing studies has traditionally valued.

With increased attention to multimodal scholarship, teaching, and composing, the question of accessibility must be at the forefront of multimodal theories and pedagogical practices. Otherwise, we are excluding large groups of people (both students and instructors) from the field. In "Multimodality in Motion: Disability and Kairotic Spaces," Cynthia Selfe and Franny Howes observe that "it is ethically questionable to practice pedagogies and construct spaces that categorically exclude entire classes of people" (Yergeau et al., "Multimodality"). An *ethics of accessibility* accounts for the material needs of both students and instructors, while recognizing the need for writing curricula to be responsible to and respectful of difference. This ethic connects to classroom practices—in the activities we develop and projects we assign—and to disciplinary scholarship and discourses about the literacies that we privilege. Accessibility is a social justice issue, and engaging an ethics of accessibility calls for critical assessment of multimodal theories and practices to ensure that multimodality is an asset rather than one more barrier for disabled students to overcome. Inviting students to *come over* to the multimodal design of pedagogical spaces—sharing how they learn best, reflecting on accessible modes and media of communication, and providing informal and formal feedback on inaccessible practices—is an active step toward resisting rhetorics of overcoming, which I address in the final section.

Universally Designing the Writing Classroom[13]

Like multimodal pedagogies that emphasize rhetorical awareness and self-reflection, the UDL Guidelines emphasize engaging students by optimizing individual choice and autonomy, increasing relevance, varying the demands and challenges of different projects, and encouraging students to self-regulate by developing self-assessment and reflection. UD emerged as an architectural theory of accessibility that foregrounds disability and disabled experiences in order to construct physical spaces that are accessible to the widest range of people possible; for example, a curb cut provides access for wheelchairs, strollers, and rolling backpacks. UD's emphasis on fixing the problems within physical environments rather than problemed individuals has been adapted for design of pedagogical environments that allow all students to access and fully engage within these spaces. The educators and instructional designers at CAST, a nonprofit organization that researches accessible technologies and pedagogical practices, have been fine-tuning the theory and practice of universal design for learning (UDL) for years.[14] The three principles of UDL—providing multiple means of engagement, representation, and action and expression—are informed by educational research that shows that learners have different motivations for learning and ways of engaging with material, they need content presented in multiple formats to aid in perception and comprehension of material, and they have different ways of expressing what they know. The core value of these principles is flexibility in teaching practices, course design, and how we engage and encourage students to learn and compose.

While universal design was developed as a framework that can be applied to any discipline or pedagogical environment, I argue that UD and its principles of providing multiple means of engagement, representation, and action and expression are integral to college writing instruction and the crafting of flexible pedagogies that account for and value the many different needs of student writers. With its valuing of social justice, different learning and composing processes, and a wide range of pedagogical theories and practices, writing studies aligns with many of the core values of UD. Many in writing studies have both considered and critiqued UD as an approach to writing instruction. Patricia Dunn and Kathleen Dunn De Mers place these two discourses in conversation in a 2002 *Kairos* webtext, exploring how intellectual work can be presented using different (nontraditional and nonalphabetic) approaches that productively challenge a wider range of students in the writing classroom. CAST's UDL Guidelines note that "it is important for all learners to learn composition, not just writing, and to learn the optimal medium for any particular content of expression and audience." The authors' argument to embrace UD is rooted in the belief that text- and print-only pedagogies are disabled and that we need to change them rather than changing our students—a firm social-model understanding of disability that resists rhetorics of overcoming. Dunn and Dunn De Mers assert that UD can help instructors "tap into various people's talents in debate, dialogue, visualization, drawing, and movement—all of which can be used to invent, organize, and revise conventional texts." UD can aid in different stages of the writing process, such as brainstorming ideas through mind maps, learning about citation practices by determining the right order and taping the pieces of the citation on the wall, or cutting up print drafts to reorganize ideas.

With its roots in disability justice, UD as a practice is necessarily radical in its rejection of deficit-oriented discourse. For example, two articles about UD and basic writing that emerged from the *Basic Writing e-Journal* in 2004 adopt a social-model approach to disability that rejects both one-size-fits-all pedagogies and universal literacy standards that justify the treatment of specific kinds of student differences as deficit (Bruch; McAlexander). Patrick Bruch advocates for creation of spaces and channels that invite students to share what they do and don't need, a feedback loop that can usefully inform curriculum design, pedagogical theories and practices, and academic understandings of disability. Creating a feedback loop is central to a pedagogy of *coming over* as it provides a proactive rather than retrofitted space for students to share their material needs and experiences—not just to be accommodated but to actively shape the design of the course.

Thus, UD is an opportunity to design curricular and programmatic practices that recognize the presence of disabled students and value their different ways of knowing, being, and composing. In "Mapping Composition: Inviting Disability in the Front Door," Jay Dolmage stresses the importance of instructors recognizing and respecting disability in order for each of our students to have equitable access to literacy, writing, and rhetorical meaning-making (15). This is in opposition to retrofitting already-built environments with accessible components—an afterthought made visible when a student needs an accommodation. A simple way to recognize and respect disability is through the syllabus: the first document that instructors and students navigate together. Tara Wood and Shannon Madden provide useful models for language to use in crafting an accessibility statement for a syllabus, and, more broadly, Anne-Marie Womack gives us a way of thinking about the syllabus as a whole more accessibly. Womack argues for centering disability in writing pedagogy through course and document design, providing universally designed strategies for crafting a syllabus that communicates the flexibility and ideological values of UD: "(1) creating accessible document design, (2) engaging students with cooperative language, and (3) empowering students through flexible course plans" (501). Flexibility is at the heart of UD, and Womack discusses integration of flexible deadlines and grading approaches. Incorporating UD can also look like scaffolding assignment sequences (engagement); presenting information through a lecture, a series of images, or a captioned video (representation); and encouraging students to use different modes and media to compose (action and expression). These strategies don't eliminate the need for institutional accommodations but do signal a shift in how instructors understand disability, accessibility, and student writing.

Despite its development as a flexible framework, UD has often been critiqued for the uncritical, apolitical ways it is discussed and applied in learning environments. A key part of this conversation is the word *universal* and how "universal" efforts frequently fail to include everyone. In a *Disability Studies Quarterly* article, Aimi Hamraie notes these limitations, writing, "Because design is a value-based activity, however, not all human variations straightforwardly count as part of the universal. When the content of the universal is unspecified, UD can slip into vague notions of 'all' or 'everyone' that assume normate users and de-center disability." Arguing that UD is good for everyone without making visible its roots in disability social justice renders the disabled *invisible* because they are just like everyone else, which focuses on the nondisabled "everyone else." Hamraie further develops this idea in their critical history of the UD movement, arguing that "despite Universal Design's origins in the work of disability activists and in disability rights efforts preceding the ADA, the term has become a popular discourse in the post-ADA world—not by centering disability as a category of marginalization but by disavowing it" (*Building* 7). Disability rights are at the core of UD, but its application has been depoliticized, shifting from disability accessibility toward discourses of access for all.

Access for all is one of the strongest appeals of UD: while it is theorized with disability at the foreground, designing for multiple kinds of disabilities—whether sensory, learning, intellectual, or emotional—results in practices that benefit nondisabled students, too. But when UD focuses on the broad experiences of all people and ignores the unique differences of students, it has the potential to render invisible disabled ways of being and composing. It is unrealistic to meet every single need through UD, but we can "open as many different channels of communication as possible, in hopes that at least one will be accessible enough for a given student to use it, and trust that our own attitudes will have much to do with student response" (Price, *Mad* 89). We can't apply UD as a one-size-fits-all checklist and hope that if all the boxes are checked, no more disability or accessibility issues will surface. Instead, UD is at its most effective when it is approached as a methodology (Hamraie, "Designing"), a framework for imagining space as "in process" and "constantly renegotiated" (Dolmage, "Mapping" 25). Pedagogical theories always need to be adapted to specific contexts, and UD can greatly improve inclusivity and accessibility when it is theorized and enacted as a set of dynamic and flexible strategies. UD resists reinforcing rhetorics of overcoming by recognizing multiple ways of learning and composing, and by being flexible with regard to students' different material needs—offering alternatives (such as taking notes with a laptop) rather than insisting that students overcome (by taking notes by hand).

LEGITIMIZING THE RHETORICAL POTENTIAL OF DISABLED COMPOSING PRACTICES

I want to reiterate the importance of both multimodality and universal design for informing the design and implementation of accessible writing pedagogies. Multimodality has the potential to be an accessible pedagogical framework but often perpetuates normative values and conceptions of rhetoric and composition. Similarly, I believe in the potentials of UD, although they are rarely actualized beyond the dynamic of universalizing experiences through an erasure of difference or diagnosing differences as deficit. In this section, I want to suggest another way to think about UD, disabled composing processes, and accessible pedagogical environments. This way of framing accessibility does not speak in terms of a universal environment; rather, it is one built with multiple access points, one that encourages different affinities between composing processes, allowing nonnormative rhetorical expressions and composing practices to emerge. The dream of a universal space replicates the erasure of difference as it moves too abstractly into the immaterial—a space where embodied differences are universalized and not rooted in the embodied experiences of disabled students. Enacting universally designed, multimodal writing pedagogies that acknowledge and privilege student writers' embodied ways of knowing and composing is an active step in the process of *coming over* to the understanding that difference is not something to be overcome but rather allows students more options for rhetorical expression. Adopting an embodied multimodal approach to writing pedagogy challenges established notions of what it means to compose a rational, cohesive, or otherwise "normal" text. It necessarily means rewriting conceptions of disabled composing processes, from deficit to legitimate literacy practices.

While I discuss this more fully in the final chapter, in this section I highlight a few composing strategies that are enabled by disabled embodiments. These strategies reject the idea that disabled composing practices are something that students need to overcome, and instead emphasize a collective understanding that disabled embodiments are full of rhetorical potential. I illustrate this first by discussing pedagogical practices and assignments that reinforce rhetorics of overcoming, and then by sharing snippets of pedagogical moments where I have tried to make space for disabled composing processes in my first-year writing classes through mind mapping, decomposition, and collaborative accessibility. Ultimately, I hope to illustrate how multimodal pedagogies that attend to both embodiment and UD offer a way to ensure accessibility that is rooted neither in diagnosis nor in universalized terms.

Overcoming the Literacy Narrative

Rhetorics of overcoming manifest and are sometimes even valued in classes where students engage in personal writing and traumatic narratives. Tara Wood identifies the personal narrative as a common first-year writing assignment that risks reinforcing rhetorics of overcoming. She asks, "If, indeed, there is an association between successful personal essays and engagement with traumatic experience, what are the implications for a student who identifies as disabled?" ("Overcoming" 38). When students are tasked with writing about traumatic experiences for class, it results in narration of a *linear* healing process that erases any sort of nontraumatic aspects of disability (43). Like the personal narrative, literacy narratives tend to follow a clean, unambiguous progression that moves away from a lack of literacy, which is positioned as undesirable and must be fixed. Many assignments can deny certain ways of knowing and being, which raises the question: *In what ways do we construct pedagogical spaces that ask students to overcome their disabilities through writing?*

To avoid designing classroom environments and assignments that ask students to overcome their disabilities through writing, how do we instead encourage students to *come over* from that trope and write in a way that reflects the complexities of disabled experiences? For example, if a student chooses to write a literacy narrative about dyslexia and how she has struggled with teachers in previous classes that involved writing, what demonstrates narrative growth? The author's process of overcoming these issues? Taking control and mastering writing despite the odds? Strategies for how to fit into an inaccessible environment? If the student still struggles with writing at the end of the narrative, is that a problem? Writing instructors often encourage students to take risks, and one way that we can resist reinforcing rhetorics of overcoming in narratives is to encourage students to challenge linear progress narratives, which often omit the lived material realities of disabled embodiments.

Mind Mapping

I teach the majority of my first-year writing courses with a disability theme, which means students read texts about disability (and by disabled writers), develop research projects related to the course inquiry, and experiment with different embodied composing processes throughout the semester. For example, I ask students to practice both traditional outlines and mind maps; we experiment with text-to-speech and speech-to-text features easily accessible through Microsoft Word and Google Docs; I facilitate multimodal workshops where students craft, collage, and compose texts related to writing; and I encourage students to compose texts in whatever medium they choose. I want to share a couple of nonnormative composing practices here as examples of *mad composing*: an act of embodying madness through the production of multimodal texts.

A few years ago, I had a student in a first-year writing course who decided to research society's misunderstandings of obsessive-compulsive disorder (OCD) for her final project, but the ideas were disconnected, underdeveloped, and focused mainly on listing diagnostic characteristics. For her multimodal text translating the argument, she disclosed her relationship with OCD by mapping two brains onto a poster board. One contained only two thought bubbles: "I need to clean my room" and "I'm sooo OCD." The second brain had sixteen thought bubbles organized with color-coded stressors, such as "I need to check the door again," "What if I throw this away and then need it?" and "I've lost control." One thought on the poster board stood out to me: "Don't ask questions. Your teacher already hates you." This text prompted me to reflect on my interactions with this student throughout the semester: the quick headshakes *no* when I asked if she had questions, anxiety about in-class writing, perfect attendance but an inconsistent history of submitting work. It also made me question my reaction to her essay—how she perceived the assignment, the evaluation criteria I provided, and goals of academic writing more broadly. By normative standards, her essay missed the mark, but the final assignment allowed her to embody her argument and combine visual and textual modes to communicate more clearly than her writing throughout the semester.

I think of this as a process of *mind mapping*: exploring messy, complex, and recursive thoughts rather than outlining linear ideas. Of course, there is mind mapping that is used as a brainstorming and outlining tool, which presents students with a different way of visualizing their ideas, whether mapped by hand or designed through an app such as Canva. But I want to imagine mind mapping more broadly as a process that disrupts normative composing processes and translates embodied knowledge into the composition of a text. For my student, that meant communicating her experiences with OCD visually, rather than trying to follow the linear discussion of diagnostic characteristics that she used to structure her essay.

Decomposition

Because of the embodied and intersectional nature of disability, my students in disability-themed first-year writing courses frequently address issues that align with their lived experiences and subjectivities for their research projects. These multimodal texts have ranged from poster boards to cardboard prostheses to texts that tackle what might be considered more *intense* disabled embodiments. Robert McRuer refers to *decomposition* as the active rejection of a standard, disembodied writing that instead draws attention to "disruptive, inappropriate, composing bodies" (155). Decomposition is an opportunity to resist normative writing practices, and is an embodied multimodal pedagogy that makes space for disabled composing processes that have been deemed inappropriate or unwelcome in spaces of higher education.

An example of decomposition is "Suicide Glitch," a video I received from a first-year writing student that explores music's effects on manic depression and suicidal ideation. It is part performance, as the student thrashes their body around an empty room as different genres of music are played, and part confessional, as the student reflects on their personal history of mental illness. As the video progresses, it decomposes: the video glitches visually and auditorily as the confessional progresses, resulting in a mass of colors and noises that are indistinguishable. The video engages in an act of decomposition by disrupting normative understandings of both composing processes and rhetorical expression. The unruly body thrashing around an empty room, clashing media elements that disrupt the narrative, and detailed reflections of mental illness are not normative rhetorical choices. This medium allowed the student to embody their discussion of mental illness and layer media to represent the overwhelming experience of depression and suicidal ideation through sensory overload. The use of video and audio contributes to and disrupts the narrative, and, because stigmas of mental illness and suicide are so deeply embedded, the content is arguably inappropriate for an academic writing classroom. By placing themselves within the text and combining video, sound, and text, this student embodies the madness of composing and of being composed.

Collaborative Accessibility

Multimodal composition and UD offer two pedagogical frameworks that can also facilitate design of physical and pedagogical space for disabled student writers, yet both theories illustrate the complexities of social-model understandings of disability. To repeat myself, there are dangers to pedagogical approaches that ignore the material needs and unique potentials of disabled student writers. Desires to normalize diverse bodies and composing processes, though different in intent, resonate with rhetorics of overcoming: When students overcome, they are normalized. When we expect students to overcome their disabilities, we expect them to reach a "normal" level of "good" writing. Thus, a universally designed, multimodal pedagogy is one that must always be reflective, adaptive, and focused on the material needs and embodied experiences of disabled student writers—in addition to the other students who would benefit from the multiple access points these practices create. Instead of spaces built on diagnosis or overgeneralized universal experiences, we need pedagogical and curricular practices that center accessibility and flip the overcoming narrative by inviting students to come over and contribute to the accessibility and inclusivity of their learning environments, a process that is always dynamic and contextual.

Accessibility is a collaborative effort, and UD emphasizes collaboration as a way to sustain student effort and persistence. It is important to create structures where students collaborate and learn with each other, and also spaces where students can collaborate with instructors and provide input on accessible writing practices. In her discussion of collaboration by difference, Cathy Davidson argues, "Collaboration by difference respects and rewards different forms and levels of expertise, perspective, culture, age, ability, and insight, treating difference not as a deficit but as a point of distinction" (100). In multimodal writing classrooms, students work to develop new understandings of writing, negotiate levels of familiarity with new modes and media, and work to create new forms of composition. Collaboration by difference encourages students with varying abilities, levels of knowledge, and areas of expertise to come together to make meaning. This collaboration must also extend to conversations between instructors and students about accessible and inclusive ways to construct learning environments, including learners in the design of the learning process:

> Support students to become an "expert" about their own learning. The goal is to find a way into the learning experience, remain persistent in the face of challenge or failure, and continue to build self-knowledge. Encourage students to communicate their learning preferences and needs. Include students in designing better learning environments. ("About UDL")

Writing instructors often include students in the design process by encouraging students to co-construct syllabus policies, establish contract grading, and choose course themes or shared inquiries. Collaboration means encouraging students to work with and learn from each other, giving them space to demonstrate their different areas of expertise, and inviting them to come over and provide feedback on inaccessible environments. A simple way to solicit feedback that doesn't put pressure on any one individual student is to distribute informal surveys throughout the semester that ask students about their access needs. Collaboration by difference is a productive means for thinking about students and instructors *coming over* to develop anti-ableist, accessible practices. UD is a process of listening and discussing, and overcoming inaccessible physical and social structures means valuing students' feedback and inviting them to come over to these conversations.

RESISTING RHETORICS OF OVERCOMING AND BUILDING ACCESSIBLE, ANTI-ABLEIST FUTURES

Engaging rhetorics of overcoming is an ableist process that positions disabled student writers and disabled embodiments as *less than* and normative composing processes as ideal. When people engage in rhetorics of overcoming, they reinforce the stigma of disability as something bad that has no place in higher education and must instead be overcome for a student to succeed within that space. These processes—from diagnosis or disclosure to remediation or accommodation—insist that disability diagnoses and impairment-specific teaching practices are not just the best but also the *only* way to support disabled student writers. This orientation to disability prevents writing instructors from imagining accessible environments that both support and encourage nonnormative expressions of rhetoricity. Resisting rhetorics of overcoming means recognizing the value of disabled embodiments, encouraging multiple ways of knowing and meaning-making, and building pedagogical structures that allow disabled student writers to claim their own agency.

Perpetuating misunderstandings about disability and disabled student writers, whether intentionally or not, has serious implications. As I noted at the outset of this chapter, well-intentioned desires to support students are often hindered by an unwillingness to base accommodation on disability theory and disabled students' experiences. Good intentions are detrimental to the collaborative work of building accessibility, because when we are motivated by intention rather than social justice and work without the direct input of those we intend to help, we risk reinforcing rhetorics of overcoming by building on theories, ideas, and assumptions that create more barriers than access points. Accessibility is collaborative and must necessarily welcome and foreground the material experiences and disabled embodiments that student writers bring to the classroom.

By tracing dominant discourses of disability in writing studies—diagnosis and remediation, accommodation, and accessibility through multimodality and UD—I hope to have shown not only how different cultural understandings of disability have manifested in our scholarship in different moments, but also how different writing studies theories and practices work to reinforce or resist rhetorics of overcoming. Just as medical and social models of disability have been challenged by DS scholars as too dichotomous and limiting of the different ways to theorize and understand disability, I hope to emphasize the complexities of how writing studies scholars have theorized disability and accessibility. In the next chapter, I further develop how rhetorics of overcoming manifest within writing center scholarship and practices, illustrating how this approach has influenced remediative consulting practices employed when students' needs are not met through normative best practices. With a history of resisting remediation, making space for voices often excluded from disciplinary scholarship, and diversifying modes of communication through teaching and composing practices, writing studies is on its way to a more accessible future. To truly build accessible, anti-ableist futures, we must ensure that disability and embodiment are central to conversations about programmatic and curricular design, teacher and tutor training, assessment, and diversity.

3

Resisting Diagnosis and Creating Avenues for Agency in the Writing Center

> Disabled students—of whatever stripe or character—are different from the non-disabled, but does that mean that they should be treated differently in the writing center? Do they deserve special considerations and specialized tutoring?
> —Michael A. Pemberton, "'Special Needs' Students and Writing Centers"

> Find a writing center that is committed to supporting students with learning or physical disabilities, and chances are you will find a center that is also conscientious, innovative, and warm.
> —Cheryl Hofstetter Towns, "Serving the Disabled in the Writing Center"

IT WAS 2012, AND I WAS attending an international writing center conference, fighting back tears as I walked out of a crowded panel session about the increasing number of students with Asperger's syndrome who frequented university writing centers. I had been listening to a presentation about some of the telltale characteristics of autism spectrum disorders and how tutors should respond to these traits. These were suggestions like, "Don't encourage outlining, because autistic writers struggle to connect their ideas," and "Autistic people have bad handwriting, so you should offer them the opportunity to use the computer." At the end of the presentation, the speaker said that Asperger's "is an obstacle that can be overcome if the student wants," adding that tutors can aid in this process. The question-and-answer session quickly became a mix of emphatic agreement and discussion of how to identify students who seem suspicious and may become violent. It was the last time I attended that conference.

This anecdote is just one of many that highlight disciplinary desires to diagnose students in order to help them overcome their disabilities. It contributes to a larger narrative that positions disability as dangerous if left undisclosed and that encourages tutors to do the diagnosing or to at least encourage students to self-disclose, reifying the idea that the writing center is a space where students can be fixed by identifying diagnostic traits that contribute to "bad" writing. From their inception as writing clinics—spaces to remediate struggling or deficient writers—writing centers have fought the remedial label. To resist this label, writing center mission statements emphasize their work as supporting students with individualized instruction that moves away from "fixing" papers and lower-order concerns and instead focuses on higher-order concerns, such as brainstorming and organizing ideas, developing clear thesis statements and arguments, and assessing credible evidence. Because of their one-on-one interactions with students, writing centers are spaces where consultants and tutors have more time with students to talk about their different writing needs, strengths, and challenges than may be possible in a classroom context.

Even though writing center ideals value students' different knowledges and composing processes, many tutoring and consulting best practices—such as the read-aloud model and nondirective questioning—are framed for students with particular abilities. The read-aloud model, for example, privileges nondisabled students who hear, speak, and can focus for long periods of time. Rebecca Day Babcock addresses these standard practices in *Tell Me How It Reads: Tutoring Deaf and Hearing Students in the Writing Center*:

> Some common writing center practices are reading the paper aloud (either by the tutor or the tutee), the concepts that the student "owns" the paper and that the tutor should neither write on the paper nor offer words and language to the tutee, and the use of nondirective questioning techniques, sometimes known as "hands-off" or "minimalist" tutoring. A nondirective question might be "Why did you put a comma

here?" rather than just telling the student the rule for using a comma. (6)

Reading aloud and nondirective strategies can be highly inaccessible for deaf students and may also create barriers for autistic students, students with pragmatic or perception impairment, and a range of students who need more structured (directive) tutoring or for whom reading aloud is less effective. Students who do not respond to these standard practices are positioned as different, sometimes dangerous, often beyond the help of peer and professional consultants—something I have observed in writing center scholarship, national and international conferences, and online writing center discussion forums. Often, consultants feel responsible to diagnose students or to persuade them to disclose so that they can recommend them to professional campus services or deny them the opportunity to discuss their writing in the same capacity as other students. Despite a disciplinary rejection of remediation and commitment to providing one-on-one literacy instruction for all students, disabled student writers are still frequently positioned as beyond the help of peer tutors—unable to overcome their disabilities and become better writers.

In this chapter, I address how rhetorics of overcoming manifest within writing center scholarship and pedagogy, and how to develop accessible practices that resist diagnosis and remediation of disabled students. Specifically, I argue that writing centers have an opportunity, given their work with students one on one, to develop pedagogical spaces that authorize writerly agency for both disabled and nondisabled students. I begin by addressing how writing center discourses have reinforced rhetorics of overcoming by emphasizing diagnosis, particularly for learning-disabled and autistic student writers. Accommodating specific diagnostic characteristics reinforces rhetorics of overcoming and leads to static practices for disabled students rather than flexible, accessible practices.

Resisting rhetorics of overcoming involves prioritizing accessibility in the theory, design, and implementation of writing center practices—rather than retrofitting existing practices for specific disability diagnoses, a process that often results in remediative pedagogies. I propose that the shift toward multimodal writing center environments creates an ideal moment to be proactive in designing learning environments that acknowledge and value the multiple, nonnormative literacies and knowledges students bring with them to writing center spaces that, like first-year writing classes, are designed to meet the needs of all university students. As in Chapter 2, I discuss the possibilities of multimodality and universal design as frameworks for designing writing center spaces and practices that engage embodied literacy practices and resist rhetorics of overcoming. Again, I argue for the importance of inviting disabled student writers to *come over* to conversations about their composing needs and, more literally, inviting folks from on-campus offices who are committed to accessibility and diversity to *come over* to writing center spaces to facilitate conversations about disability and accessibility. Finally, I conclude by reflecting on writing centers as models for what it means to create multiple avenues—or access points—for writers to express themselves, without a reliance on diagnosis.

DISCOURSES OF DIAGNOSIS, REMEDIATION, AND ACCOMMODATION

Writing center administrators are eager to adapt to student and institutional needs in order to counter perceptions of these spaces as unnecessary or remedial. Writing center consultants, even more than first-year writing instructors, must be willing and equipped to support a range of students, from first-year to graduate students, as well as nonnative speakers and disabled students. This support necessitates flexible and adaptable pedagogical practices. When adaptive responses develop from a defensive place or a place of anxiety, though, "we repeat patterns rather than change orientation" (Grimm, "Rearticulating" 534). And there is certainly a lot of anxiety about disability, which often leads to instructors, administrators, and consultants prioritizing diagnosis as a way to learn about students' needs. This turn toward diagnostic criteria as definitive guidelines for working with disabled student writers does more harm than good, as the resulting practices reinforce the pattern of diagnosis, accommodation, and cure. Indeed, writing center discourses about disability are deeply entrenched in medical-model understandings of disability. As I described in Chapter 2, medicalized approaches to disability insist that students' individual deficits must be treated or cured, if possible. In the writing center, this coincides with a remediation model of tutoring that relies on diagnosis and individual accommodations that treat those medical symptoms and not necessarily the dynamic needs of students. In this section, I address writing center discourses that reinforce rhetorics of overcoming through diagnosis, remediation, and accommodation, drawing attention to the ways in which the erasure of disabled students' agency is a result of scholarship that is reliant on the historical impulse to diagnose and help. I present diagnostic approaches to disability specific to learning disabilities, autism, and deafness—not to highlight what has been learned about the diagnostic characteristics, but instead to illustrate how these approaches erase the agency of disabled student writers.

Like writing studies instructors and scholars, writing center administrators began discussing learning disabilities in the 1980s, a few years after Section 504 legislation required institutions of higher education to provide equal access for disabled college students.[15] The question everyone had, though, was, *How do we adapt practices to account for the needs of LD students?* LD first appeared as its own topic (rather than a passing reference) in 1984 in *The Writing Lab Newsletter*, when George Gleason solicited advice from other practitioners about how to work with dyslexic students. Gleason describes his approach, which involves talking to students about their particular kind of dyslexia: "If I knew more about your kind, I might be able to help you—or to tell you where you can get help. But frankly, you can't be too bad off or you would probably not have made it into college" (6). He also mentions that building students' confidence by meeting with them regularly is important "to refine diagnosis and to devise remedies" (6). These examples do not demonstrate an absolute refusal to work with dyslexic students. Indeed, Gleason's first step is to talk with students about their learning needs and to check in with them periodically, but those needs are confined within the diagnosis rather than students' lived experiences. Gleason makes clear that he is only inquiring about mild dyslexics, because severe dyslexics are "another matter; they have difficulties I don't know how to address, so I send them to experts" (7). Again, this statement emphasizes the need to distinguish mild from severe dyslexics and the expertise needed to work with dyslexic students.[16] Gleason ends his brief article with a question, "How do others deal with such special people?" (7), which prompted a discussion that continued into the early 1990s. The writing center scholars and practitioners involved in this conversation wanted to identify issues with specific disabilities in order to better serve students, but focusing on diagnosing and identifying practices for disabled students contributes to the rhetorics of overcoming so prevalent in writing center discourse.

Rhetorics of overcoming are perpetuated, first, through a lack of basic knowledge of and familiarity with disability and disabled student writers that is then exacerbated by the assurance and insistence that writing center staff should occupy the role of disability expert when making decisions about what disabled student writers need. The process of diagnosis and remediation emphasizes difference, not as natural but as something special and different from what writing center folks can reasonably accommodate. All students who enter a writing center are treated individually and, thus, as *different* from one another in terms of what they bring to the center: the assignment and their interpretation of it, their writing and rhetorical ability, how they learn and compose. The problem, then, is not positioning disabled students as different or as individuals. What is troubling is the idea that disabled students are treated so differently that they must be diagnosed and work with tutors who have specialized knowledge about disability.[17] Perhaps even more troubling is when tutors and administrators determine that disabled student writers are beyond help. These disability discourses create an either/or binary, where tutors must be experts or they can't work with disabled student writers—which leaves no room for the input of disabled student writers who *are* often experts in their learning and writing needs.

Medical-model approaches to disability operate under the assumption that disabled students are so radically different from other students that they are beyond the help of the writing center—that they require too much time, resources, or special knowledge. An example of medical-model discourse is Steve Sherwood's 1996 article, "Apprenticed to Failure: Learning from the Students We Can't Help." In a reflection on a failed session, he writes, "I had no training in helping students cope with learning disabilities, much less with the effects of a severe brain injury" (49), concluding that we will continue to encounter LD students who "despite our best efforts, we can't help" (56). Sherwood argues that tutors are not trained to work with LD students and that writing centers are not designed to help LD students.[18] Tanya Titchkosky describes this as a "you can't accommodate everybody" attitude in higher education that deems specific bodies "'naturally' a problem for some spaces" (35). The argument that disabled students are completely beyond the help of writing centers is not the predominant narrative in writing center discourses of disability; however, scholarship that relies on diagnosis, identifiable disability traits, and scientific expertise has significant medical-model undertones that have been reified through the articles that are reprinted in guides for writing center directors and tutors.

While there are discourses of diagnosis, remediation, and—more severely—refusal to work with disabled students, most writing center scholarship focuses on accommodation. An accommodation approach to accessibility attempts to meet students' needs by identifying the specific characteristics of a disability in order to adapt tutoring or consulting practices for a specific student. For example, in her anthologized essay, "Learning Disabilities and the Writing Center," Julie Neff outlines pedagogical practices that could help LD students, beginning with a medical overview of the biological and neurological causes of LD and supporting her discussion with a case study that creates overgeneralizations about LD students—for example, that they lack the spatial awareness to drive a car or to remove the plastic wrap before roasting a chicken. Though Neff is well intentioned, convinced that writing centers can serve the needs of LD student writers, who she admits are intelligent and resourceful (382), the reliance on assigning practices based on overgeneralized diagnostic characteristics reinforces rhetorics of overcoming by asking LD students to respond to these practices positively—even if they do not take into consideration students' material needs. Like a diagnostic checklist, this becomes a way to normalize writing behaviors by providing a quick fix for each disability characteristic.

These discourses reflect cultural understandings of disability as deficit or personal tragedy—understandings that are by no means unique to writing centers, yet influence current writing center discourses and practices for working with disabled student writers. For example, Neff's article was originally published in 1994 but has been reprinted and anthologized, and many report—through journal articles, conferences, and the Wcenter listserv—that they use it as representative text for tutoring LD students. This and other articles reflect outdated and overgeneralized understandings of LD students, yet they are circulated as examples of disability scholarship and taught in tutor training classes, extending the influence of these attitudes. Throughout writing studies discourse is a tension in folks wanting to help students but not knowing *how*, which illustrates the need for DS approaches to accessibility, different types of learning and composing processes, and talking openly with students about their needs.

I am frequently told that disabled students do not know their needs or how they learn best, which dismisses their writerly agency. But is this true? Thanks in large part to the passing of disability legislation like the Individuals with Disabilities Education Act (IDEA) and a familiarity with special education programs, disabled college students are often "savvy about their rights and insistent on their needs for instructional accommodation" (Hawkes 372).[19] In her chapter in *The Writing Center Director's Resource Book*, Lory Hawkes acknowledges, that writing center staff are often unsure how best to negotiate students' legal accommodations:

> Hampered in part by a personal lack of understanding of this emerging population and in part by an institutional void in which there is no coherent, articulated institutional policy on educating the disabled student, well-intentioned writing center staff may resort to tried and true methods of composition

review and revision in face-to-face encounters that simply do not work for disabled students. (374)

This uncertainty manifests in rhetorics of overcoming: the good intentions, the need to either know the disability or have scholarship (i.e., expertise) that guides the tutor, and a default to inaccessible practices—not because the consultant is not trying, but because they are unsure of what to do. Hawkes also takes an accommodation approach to technology, pushing for increased access to assistive technologies specifically to help students overcome disability-related writing struggles through "compensating" and "remediating" practices (377). The mix of legal obligation and reliance on assistive technologies to remediate emphasizes the many ways that disabled students are treated differently.

More recently, rhetorics of overcoming through diagnosis and accommodation have manifested strongly in discourses of autism in the writing center, like the example I provided at the beginning of this chapter. It is unsurprising that autism is receiving attention in writing center discourse, given the larger cultural and academic discourses that circulate about it, and—although accommodating tendencies and medical-model desires to diagnose are still quite prevalent—more socially just cultural understandings of accommodating disability are prevalent, too. In 2008, Terry Collins prompted a discussion about autism in *The Writing Lab Newsletter* by identifying common behaviors attributed to Asperger's, such as students avoiding eye contact and stimming, and advocating for accommodating rather than remediating these behaviors. Because these characteristics are so subtle, though, "writing tutors may have to rely largely on their experience and intuition to make judgments whether or not a writer might benefit from some of the following strategies proposed for those with Asperger's or other related learning disorders" (Collins 14). Tutors are encouraged to use their experiences, but if they don't share disabled experiences or have negative assumptions or stereotypes connected to those experiences, what can they rely on for engaging inclusively and accessibly?

Disabled students may have learning and composing practices that are much different from consultants' own experiences, so it is important not to position consultants as experts. In "Serving the Disabled in the Writing Center," Cheryl Hofstetter Towns argues:

> Tutors must not view them-selves as "saviors" out to rescue "poor, help-less" disabled students. Disability does not equal inability. A tutor's job is to tutor each disabled student as any other student, perhaps providing a few necessary accommodations and fostering independence as much as possible. Empower, don't rescue. (15–16)

Towns advocates for writing center staff to treat disabled students fairly, to make writing center spaces and practices more accessible, and to be direct about meeting disabled students' needs—relying on the expertise of the students themselves. Inviting disabled student writers to come over and share their experiences and needs is integral to designing environments that are accessible and inclusive, rather than just accommodating.

Shifting the culture of accessibility in writing centers involves being mindful of disability and creating spaces to address attitudes and understandings of disability, which begins with tutor training. Tutor training is an important space for educating consultants about strategies that enable student agency and approach disability from a cultural framework rather than a diagnostic one. In her discussion of autism, April Mann suggests that we do not benefit from simply identifying student difference in the writing center; rather, "progress will come through learning to understand commonalities and through developing and promulgating strategies which acknowledge and encourage the abilities of the students in the [Asperger's] population" (46). Many writing center practices equip consultants to help disabled students, such as chunking assignments into manageable parts, helping students set reasonable assignment goals, and encouraging and fostering intellectual engagement. However, there are also cultural differences that make highly regarded writing center practices inaccessible. For example, in *Tell Me How It Reads: Tutoring Deaf and Hearing Students in the Writing Center*, one of Babcock's deaf participants, Rae, notes that folks in Deaf culture do not benefit from nondirective tutoring strategies and advises tutors to be patient, clear, and understanding of deaf students whose first language is not English.[20] The need for education about disability culture is echoed by one of the hearing tutors, Gustav, who notes, "What's most important for me is to have more exposure to different people with different disabilities, with different language, different modes of communication" (Babcock, *Tell* 73).[21] Educating consultants about accessible writing center strategies and disability culture allows for a student-centered practice that moves beyond accommodations that are based on one-dimensional, static understandings of disability.

SUPPORTING MULTIPLE LITERACIES AND PROMOTING AGENTIVE LEARNING

In this section, I want to address accessible practices that do not require diagnosis, that refuse rhetorics of overcoming, and that recognize the value of nonnormative literacy practices. Specifically, I address some of the initiatives that writing centers are taking up in terms of multiliteracies and multimodal practices that both encourage the multiple literacies that students bring with them to the writing center and create access points that promote agentive learning. As writing centers shift toward multimodal environments, it is necessary to design learning environments that acknowledge and value the nonnormative literacies and knowledges that students bring with them to writing center spaces. As in Chapter 2, I argue that multimodal practices can greatly increase accessibility but are not inherently accessible or anti-ableist, and I address the potentials of universal design as a way to enable disabled students' agency.

Engaging Multiliteracies and Multimodal Literacies

Like writing studies, writing center discourses are moving toward social-justice-oriented theorizing of writing center practices, and many writing center applications of this are technologically and multimodally driven. In 2000, John Trimbur noted the socially just values undergirding multiliteracies, writing, "Linked to the notion of multiliteracies is the challenge to develop more equitable social futures by redistributing the means of communication" (30). An institutional push toward valuing and encouraging students' multiple literacies—rather than standard academic literacy—creates opportunities for students whose literate practices have been historically ignored, undervalued, or targeted for remedial practices. More than a decade ago, the New London Group theorized multiliteracies as an opportunity to move beyond the dominating limitations of print- and word-based literacies, recognizing the value of different modes of representation, such as visual, aural, gestural, spatial, and multimodal (28). Gunther Kress observes that these other modes are embodied, that "human bodies have a wide range of means of engagement with the world" that are employed in various ways (184). A multiliteracies pedagogy, then, encourages practices that reinforce and value students' different bodily experiences and promote student agency (New London Group 31). The development of multiliteracy centers—writing centers with initiatives to support students' multiple literacies, spaces that are "equal to the diversity of semiotic options composers have in the 21st century" (Sheridan 6)—presents an opportunity to position disability and nonnormative learning or composing practices not as things that must be overcome but as assets. Multiliteracy centers, according to David Sheridan, "should facilitate the competent and critically reflective use of technologies and other material, institutional, and cultural resources" (6). The use of technologies is not a universal solution but can provide valuable composing opportunities for disabled students.

With their focus on composing, writing center scholars have always been invested in the potentials of computers and technology to aid in the composing processes of all students, particularly those with disabilities. For example, a technology as simple as the tape recorder is a means to increase accessibility for dyslexic, blind, and mobility-impaired students (Towns 14). More recently, writing center spaces have integrated computers and added computer labs, which requires attention to physical accessibility, because retrofitting or denying access to disabled students is not an option: "You cannot, for example, send wheelchair students into a separate room because your predecessor has not allowed enough space for them in the existing lab" (Berta 6). There are many benefits to incorporating accessible technologies into learning spaces, particularly for disabled students. For example, Helen Quinn and Carole Flint observed that their Technical Communication Resource Center and Writing Lab allowed LD students "to leave their frustrations behind and realize their full potential as mature and intelligent writers. Not only is the computer a patient, objective 'tutor,' allowing the students to make repeated revisions, but it also is nonthreatening" (11). The ease of typing facilitates drafting and revising, and detracts from lower-order concerns like spelling and handwriting.[22] Access to computers does not ensure accessibility but is necessary for creating environments where students have support for both computing and composing.

Online tutoring also presents opportunities to provide access for disabled students while meeting the goals of a multiliteracy center. For example, in "Expanding the Space of f2f," M. Remi Yergeau et al. explore synchronous audio-video-textual (AVT) conferencing as a "semiotically rich medium that sustains critical 'social cues' and enhances interaction and exchange." AVT conferencing is different from online tutoring via email because it is conducted in real time and uses different and multiple modes. Yergeau et al. argue that "with its integration of video, audio, still image, and text, AVT conferencing extends Trimbur's (2000) call for multimodal communication, inevitably engaging student learners with more than 'just' print literacy." The AVT interface is a rich space that promotes technological literacy, allows students to compose multimodally, and gives them options for communicating in different ways. A digital interface offers both rhetorical and physical accessibility for students who cannot be physically present in the writing center, perhaps because of the inaccessibility of the writing center space, a chronic illness, or an anxiety disorder that makes it difficult for the student to commit to a physical appointment.

Often, *multiliteracies* refers to the different technological abilities, or literacies, that a person has for communicating through electronic means. Writing centers encourage these literacies by housing computer labs, giving students access to specialized video and editing software, and creating online writing labs. However, increased access to technology does not necessarily indicate greater accessibility, and a focus on multiple literacies that only prioritizes digital literacies can exclude both students and centers that lack access to these technological resources.[23] If we conceive of multiliteracies more broadly, as *embodied* practices (as Kress does), students have access to multiple and flexible options for engaging in tutoring sessions, such as a blind student who relies on auditory and sensory modes or a deaf student who relies on visual modes. Emphasizing the different modes of composing through a multimodal pedagogy recognizes students as "agentive, resourceful and creative meaning-makers" (Stein 122). This agentive learning is valuable for students to take control of how they best receive and create knowledge, and writing centers are known for supporting multimodal practices and active, student-centered learning. Engaging in multimodal tutoring practices—that include but extend beyond understandings of multimodality and multiliteracies as necessarily tied to digital technology—allows for richer pedagogical accessibility.[24] With its emphasis on multiplicity and flexibility, a multimodal pedagogy adapts to students' different access needs.

Universally Designing Writing Center Pedagogy

While multimodal infrastructures create access points for a diverse range of students, they do not ensure accessibility without attention to DS and the embodied and material needs of disabled student writers. As a framework, UD advocates for multiple and flexible modes while centering disability and accessibility in ways that multimodality does not on its own. Enacting UD requires building accessible spaces, and though some spaces are redesigned to support multiple rooms and new technologies, a writing center does not need to change completely to implement accessible practices. This is demonstrated with the multiplicity and flexibility of spatial configurations: tables and chairs with wheels, cubicles or open spaces, overstuffed chairs, and computer stations. Even something as simple as decor or furniture arrangement can shape how students create meaning. And while spatial elements are important, they should not be separated from a writing center's pedagogical goals. Indeed, James Inman warns that many writing center spaces are designed around things—furniture and technology—rather than practices (20). The physical spaces we inhabit affect our actions within those spaces; in turn, our actions and social practices affect those spaces (Lefebvre). The material spaces of writing centers influence the pedagogy those spaces enact, and students do not benefit from inaccessible practices even within an accessible space. Universal design for learning offers a framework for extending the equitable and flexible spatial principles of UD to our writing pedagogies. Theorizing multimodal practices with UD can inform the development of accessible practices for working with disabled students and students with nonnormative literacies that are grounded in disability theory instead of localized interactions with students.

While the *universal* in *universal design* might suggest otherwise, design of accessible environments must always account for the specific context of a writing center: who it serves, the layout of the space, the practices that staff and institution can support, etc. An accessibility audit that takes stock of the physical and pedagogical environment, and whether there are physical or pedagogical barriers that exclude disabled student writers, is a great first step in resisting rhetorics of overcoming. For example, Nancy Grimm reflects on how her writing center staff relied on research firmly situated in the medical model when LD students first started frequenting her writing center, "implicating the student's memory as a static diseased entity. The instruction that results from this model is decontextualized rote training" ("Tutoring" 337). The rote exercises that emerged from this research were neither appropriate nor useful for students. After an accessibility check, Grimm was able to identify more inclusive practices for disabled student writers in her university writing center and redesign the center's approach to accessibility. Designing pedagogies that prioritize students' material needs and value students' embodied modes of engaging, learning, and composing are key to ensuring accessibility.

While UD has not been a central focus of writing center scholarship related to disability and accessibility, there have been some writing center discourses on the subject in the last ten years. Notably, Jean Kiedaisch and Sue Dinitz offer a clear model for applying UD to writing center training and theory. Responding to tutors' negative reactions toward LD students, Kiedaisch and Dinitz decided to redirect tutor training, "changing [their] approach to diversity from a focus on difference to a focus on identity" (45) by recruiting more diverse tutors, assigning readings that addressed multiple perspectives, and requiring tutors to reflect on everyday praxis. They invited a disabilities specialist from their university's support services to come over and talk to tutors about the harm in developing specific practices for disabled students, given that all students come to writing centers with different knowledges and abilities (50). This may seem counterintuitive for writing center pedagogies that are so focused on individualized instruction, but Kiedaisch and Dinitz use the principles of UD to outline a pedagogy that is flexible, collaborative, and accessible. They advocate for adjusting our assumptions about students' abilities, and reposition disability through a social theoretical lens that allows them to do more local, reflective work without overgeneralizing disabled experiences. This article illustrates how good practices can be reinforced by DS theory, providing a model for addressing disability more constructively within tutor training and consulting sessions.

Although Kiedaisch and Dinitz make the clearest theoretical case for paying attention to UD and collaborating with institutional disability support services when considering accessible practices, others have also advocated for this (Hamel; Hewett). Partnering with disability support services encourages us to rethink disability and accessibility in order to create more inclusive spaces and tutoring practices. Reporting on a 2009 survey on the invisible work of writing centers—"non-tutoring work" related to resources and services, publications, research and assessment, and collaboration with other academic units—Rebecca Jackson and Jackie Grutsch McKinney note that 38 percent (54 of 141) of institutions surveyed collaborated with their institution's Office of Disability Services. This integration of DS and collaboration with disability support services chart a more inclusive path for writing center scholarship, which is particularly important as centers move toward multimodal practices that push against the "'natural' exclusion" of disability within academia (Titchkosky 6). Kiedaisch and Dinitz ground their arguments using disability theory, illustrating how we treat students as *different* but should not treat disabled students *differently*. Collaborating with other academic units (such as disability support services), shifting our assumptions about disabled students, and focusing on accessibility and support—rather than accommodation or remediation—are necessary for working with a range of diverse, twenty-first-century learners.

The average writing center session inherently encourages a multiplicity of communicative and learning styles: students enter a center, meet with a tutor, and engage with texts in a variety of ways. These interactions may include engaging in verbal discussions, collaboratively drafting, looking up information in books, working on computers, or participating in online appointments. Still, working with such a diverse group of students on widely varying rhetorical projects can be difficult. Patricia Dunn and Kathleen Dunn De Mers admit, "Coming up with alternate strategies that simulate (and stimulate) the complex brain work involved in writing is very difficult—partly because we're so steeped in 'writing' as a heuristic for other writing, and partly because in this society we're so steeped in a narrow view of what is 'normal.'" For a peer or professional tutor, developing accessible strategies can be difficult if they have never experienced similar pedagogical practices or have not been directly affected by inaccessible practices. Therefore, it is crucial for writing center folks to develop *multimodal toolkits*—collections of flexible and adaptable multimodal practices—that enable them to adapt to different communicative interactions and provide student writers with agency to make decisions about what works for them.

MULTIMODAL TOOLKITS: COLLECTING ACCESSIBLE, FLEXIBLE PRACTICES

I'd like to imagine a pedagogical and material space that is committed to student agency. What if, instead of following a set script or applying accommodating practices based on disability diagnosis, the goal of engaging with disabled and nonnormative student writers is to create multiple access points for creating and sharing knowledge? One way to do this is by designing anti-ableist, accessible multimodal practices that are rooted in principles of UD and different embodied experiences. Developing a multimodal toolkit involves developing rhetorical strategies that are flexible and present more communicative opportunities for students. As early as 1992, Shoshana Beth Konstant argued that we do not need to present all sensory options to disabled students but should be flexible, depending on individual students and sessions. As if sensing the frustration that tutors feel in difficult sessions, Konstant writes, "Don't despair. Try something else. Have patience; the student is infinitely more frustrated than you are. Try every possible way you can think of to get your message across and if they all fail, then try something else" (6). Again, the idea is not to max out all sensory options but to provide flexibility. Konstant suggests using multiple channels to work with students: "Use combinations of visual, auditory, and kinesthetic techniques—the multisensory approach. Say it and draw it; read text aloud; use color to illustrate things" (7). Everyone has learning practices that work best for them, and consultants need to be prepared to try a variety of multimodal strategies.

The writing center at the university where I work has a laminated handout at each table with options for visual, auditory, and tactile methods of tutoring to ensure pedagogical accessibility, as well as atmospheric and seating considerations to ensure physical accessibility. It's a low-tech way to engage a multimodal, universally designed pedagogy and requires a negotiation between tutor and student—a process of coming over that invites students to discuss how they best learn and compose. Drawing from her work with deaf students, Babcock suggests explicit dialogue: "Most of all, try to find out what the deaf person needs and wants out of the session, and gear your tutoring toward that" (*Tell* 35). If students are unaware of what they want or need, knowing some multimodal practices can be useful.

A multimodal toolkit does not eliminate the need to identify students' individual needs, just as universal design does not eliminate the need for accommodations. Instead, both multimodality and UD ask us to acknowledge that all students have multiple ways of learning and knowing, and to be flexible in responding to those different needs. If a student needs to draw, the tutor can adapt and ask the student to sketch an outline of their main ideas. Similarly, talking through a text can be more beneficial than reading it word for word. McKinney encourages talking—rather than reading—as a way to interact more holistically with all features of a multimodal text ("New Media Matters" 39). This practice is useful for compositions that consist of more than just alphabetic text, and can directly benefit disabled students. For example, reading a paper aloud for errors is not always effective or appropriate when working with deaf students, students with ADHD, or students with pragmatic language impairment. It may also be inaccessible for tutors. I do not have any processing disabilities, but I struggle to engage and retain auditory information. When I worked in writing centers that enforced read-aloud policies, I would read the essay aloud and then quickly, quietly, and often ineffectively re-read it in order to process the information. By talking *about* a text, students and tutors have more opportunities to engage with the text in ways that reflect overall comprehension and understanding of their rhetorical choices.

To engage in accessible writing center practices, tutors must adapt to students' different embodied practices, recognizing that all students who enter the writing center will learn and compose in different ways for different purposes. Tutors should not be expected to be technology experts to engage in these practices, but they should have basic understandings of different modes and media for rhetorical communication. Many centers support various technologies, so it is useful to know how to locate resources online, work with software to compose multimedia texts or communicate with students who use assistive technologies, and even create audio recordings of sessions that students can replay once they leave the center. Beyond available technologies, however, Teddi Fishman reminds us that "the ability to adapt [is] more critical than any particular or specific accommodation" (65).

Adaptation is key, and this is an emerging trend of writing center scholarship about disability. For example, in 2015, *Praxis* published a special issue called "Dis/Ability in the Writing Center." The scholarship in this issue departs significantly from much of the work written about disability, because there are not any articles that advocate for specific practices for specific diagnoses. Instead, there is a thread of advocating for UD practices, hiring disabled tutors and directors, and discussing disability in tutor training courses. Many of the contributors to this special issue push back on demands for diagnosis and disclosure within the writing center:

> One of the most important things to remember when working with a student with a disability . . . is that *they know themselves best*. This means that no matter what we've read about that disability, we should defer to the student because that student's preferences and self-knowledge are far more important than their disability. In fact, I will even go so far as to say that disclosure is not even a necessary part of the conversation when working with a student with a disability. (Rinaldi)

It is remarkable to see how the narratives of disability in writing center discourses have shifted and how, as the newest writing center journal, *Praxis* is positioning itself as more socially progressive in how it discusses disability, particularly in terms of disclosure. In their discussion of creating safe spaces for tutors, Degner et al. write, "We argue that writing centers . . . have this obligation to create safe spaces in which tutors can disclose about hidden disabilities *if they choose*" (emphasis added). Disclosure is not positioned as a necessity but as something that could be useful for disabled tutors.

Indeed, Molly McHarg, a disabled student tutor, argues that "many tutors have reservations about disclosing such information, myself included. Some may be concerned that they will no longer be perceived as competent professionals" (14). Disclosure is not easy, whether you are a tutor, administrator, or student, and requiring disclosures in the writing center is both unethical and unnecessary.

Brainstorming how to craft accessible, multimodal practices may seem overwhelming. Many argue that they lack the expertise to work with disabled students—which may be particularly true in a writing center staffed by peer tutors—but when attention shifts away from prescribed practices that accommodate specific disabilities and toward flexible, multimodal practices, consultants do not need disability-specific expertise. Consultants may be hesitant to spend what already feels like a condensed session doing multimodal work when students are composing traditional academic essays. However, multimodal strategies have value in many traditional writing situations: brainstorming ideas, outlining essays or reports, and revising the organization of ideas. Though students may not be composing multimodal texts, there is value in engaging the multimodal processes of learning, brainstorming, and developing ideas. All students have a variety of rhetorical, intellectual, and physical abilities, and writing center spaces and practices must be ready to adapt to students' pedagogical and material needs.

MOVING TOWARD INCLUSIVE THEORIES AND PRACTICES

As an organization of writing center professionals and those involved in writing center activity, the International Writing Centers Association (IWCA) holds that all writing centers should:

1. Make every effort to include all writers and staff by enacting communication that takes into account various learning styles or ways of processing language. We believe that people with disabilities should be accommodated and welcomed in the writing center not only as recipients of services but also as people who work in writing centers;
2. take positive steps to ensure that our physical and virtual layouts and materials such as handouts are welcoming and accessible—not merely legally acceptable, but thoughtfully, accommodatingly, and graciously accessible, since writing centers should adequately serve both those who disclose their disabilities and those who don't;
3. remain current and familiar with disability issues (including the standards followed by local government and other organizations/institutions) and be involved with disability officers

at their institutions; be aware that varying estimates show 15 percent or more of the population is disabled and people with disabilities are considered "the population's largest minority." ("Position Statement" 1)

In 2006, IWCA published this position statement on disability to promote accommodation of disabled students, encourage multimodal tutoring practices, and advocate for accessible spaces and materials because "writing centers should adequately serve *both those who disclose their disabilities and those who don't*" (1, emphasis added). The position statement also declares IWCA's commitment to encourage disability scholarship, make conferences and publications more accessible, and better account for the needs of disabled student writers "so that discriminatory and inaccessible policies and procedures can be identified and eliminated" (2). Yet the dominant discourse in writing center scholarship about disability is deeply entrenched in rhetorics of overcoming that seek to diagnose and remediate disabled students. This is not often a refusal to work with disabled students but a lack of understanding about how to best work with any students who do not conform to standard writing center practices. To craft more accessible multimodal practices, we need to circulate more research about the accessibility of writing center spaces and practices that are rooted in disability theory and the lived experiences of students.

Writing center studies is paying more attention to disability, and it is important to be reflexive and critical of disability discourses and how the theories we read and engage with influence our pedagogical practices, because the urge to categorize students and writing center practices based on medical diagnoses remains. In a 2015 *Praxis* special issue, Babcock maps writing center scholarship about disability, categorizing a small fraction of the available literature by the method used and disability addressed. Identifying and sorting articles based on their disability categorizations necessarily means that this collection of literature approaches disability from an impairment model, because any articles adopting UD cannot fit within this framework. As we continue to diversify writing center discussions about disability, the texts and corresponding ideologies that we circulate and cite also contribute to the narratives we continue to write about disability.²⁵

I offer a range of theories and practices in this chapter—not to argue that anyone need know and implement all of them, but to contribute ideas to readers' rhetorical toolkits and offer ethical strategies for working with disabled students. Theories of multiliteracies, multimodality, and UD all offer frameworks that can inform disciplinary knowledge of how disabled and nonnormative student writers learn and compose. Ultimately, I hope to have shown strategies for moving beyond a diagnosis approach to accessibility that reinforces rhetorics of overcoming. Designing writing center environments that move beyond diagnosis and toward practices that affirm students' writerly agency is a process of *coming over*: inviting students to share their learning and composing needs at the beginning of sessions, inviting folks from disability support services to facilitate discussions of accessibility during staff meetings, and even inviting disabled student (and tutor) panelists to share their experiences.

I imagine one takeaway from this chapter could be that I am against students disclosing in the writing center, and this is simultaneously true and untrue. I have had many students disclose to me, and it has been useful, but it has been useful specifically because they disclosed to direct our time together. When students disclose to me, it is most often within the context of "I have [insert disability]. It would really help me if we did [this thing]. Can we do that instead?" As illustrated throughout this chapter, desires for diagnosis and disclosure in writing center sessions have an entrenched history in writing center scholarship. These desires connect to the need to know if students will react positively to standard practices, which aligns with the accommodation process. It is often the case in both writing classroom and writing center environments that instructors and administrators agree to change pedagogical practices only once a student presents us with formal notice of disability. When we focus on diagnosing students or persuading them to disclose to us, we assume we know what to do with that information and will do what is best for them. Unfortunately, what commonly happens at this step is either a one-size-fits-all approach that assumes all students with a certain disability learn a certain way, or a referral to Disability Services, which positions students as unable to be helped in this space.

Applying theories of UD can create a physically accessible space for a diverse student population, establishing a foundation for flexible tutoring practices and a valuing of disabled learning and composing processes. Although practices influenced by UD and multimodality can support students' different physical abilities, modes of learning, types of knowledges, and literacies, neither multimodality nor UD eliminates the need for accommodations; rather, they ask us to acknowledge the range of students who have multiple ways of learning and knowing, and to be flexible in responding to those different needs. Considering the principles of UD can also assist in development of practices that resist rhetorics of overcoming; for example, if read-aloud policies are inaccessible to some students but are still applied as a one-size-fits-all approach, disabled students are expected to overcome in order to engage the session. Adopting a UD approach to designing writing center spaces and practices, though, resists rhetorics of overcoming by acknowledging students' wide range of literacy practices and creating space that authorizes writerly agency for both disabled and nondisabled student writers.

4

Guaranteeing Access(ibility) in the Multimodal Writing Classroom

> Access, as we've come to represent it in the field, functions as a narrative of remediation and erasure. Within disability contexts, much of our scholarship positions access(ibility) as a project of rehabilitation. That is, there is a set of able-bodied *us*'s eagerly waiting to rescue a few, rare disabled *thems* who are in dire need of help.
> —M. Remi Yergeau, "Multimodality in Motion"

ON THE FIRST DAY OF A COURSE on universal design in higher education that I took in graduate school, the professor entered the room, spun in a circle, flicked the lights on and off, then walked to the desk at the front of the room. After thirty minutes of introducing herself and the course, she asked us to write down what had happened so far in the class. I jotted some notes about the syllabus content. Others in the class commented on the instructor's unusual behavior when she entered the room. Although we all experienced the same event, we interpreted and represented it differently, which was evident in how we wrote our descriptions—narratively or as bulleted lists—and what content we included, such as information on the syllabus, what the instructor had said, or observations about other students and the room. This professor's exercise emphasized the importance of accounting for how different people access the same content or environment—an introductory lesson in thinking about UD, accessibility, and different forms of meaning-making.

For me, the most significant lesson from this exercise was that accessibility is a collaborative process that requires multiple perspectives to guarantee access to information. One way that I started practicing this in my teaching was through collaborative note-taking. The idea is simple: each class, multiple students take notes and post them on the course website for others to access.[26] Collaborative note-taking offers an alternative participation option to speaking in class, gives students low-stakes practice in taking notes, becomes a shared resource that students can reference throughout the semester, and ultimately reinforces the notion that accessible practices benefit all students. Note-taking is one of the few areas of accommodation that apply to writing classes, and collaborative note-taking addresses that need while also making it a shared responsibility rather than focusing on the *one* student who requires it. Student note-takers usually undergo training to ensure that they include the appropriate information to meet the requirements of students' accommodations. Thus, collaborative note-taking also has an important ethical component because, as I have argued previously, UD does a disservice when it is framed only as *access for all* and erases the material needs of disabled student writers. It is necessary, then, to emphasize the ethical nature of collaborative note-taking and accessible practices more broadly.

Because it shifts the focus away from individual accommodations, collaborative note-taking is one way that I try to make space for *coming over*—that is, moving away from a diagnostic model of deficit and individual accommodations, and instead creating multiple access points for student engagement and emphasizing that diverse forms of meaning-making are assets. It has become a space in my classes that allows for nonnormative expressions of rhetoricity: students can participate textually rather than verbally, use color and incorporate images (of the board but also of memes) to supplement the text, draw comics of what occurs in class and then upload them to the document, and format their notes as playscripts. One student even took notes using only hashtags! Collaborative note-taking is just one way to encourage these different composing practices and forms of expression, and I will detail more throughout this chapter.

Building on the discussions of accommodation approaches to disability in Chapters 2 and 3 (in writing classrooms and writing centers, respectively), this chapter continues the narrative of moving away from a diagnostic, individual accommodation approach and toward a multiplicity of agentive practices that allow students to choose, engage, and create texts that fully articulate their insights. Guaranteeing accessibility is an ethical responsibility, and it is deeply unethical for educators to position accessibility as an afterthought, especially in multimodal writing classrooms that—in many cases—already have infrastructures for students to engage and compose in ways that emphasize their rhetorical agency. There is a significant difference between multimodal practices that accommodate certain students and multimodal practices that fully incorporate accessibility, and, as in previous chapters, I address the potentials of multimodality and UD as frameworks for designing accessible pedagogical infrastructures. I focus specifically on the multimodal writing classroom here, because multimodality can be a channel through which multiple nonnormative expressions of rhetoricity are recognized and valued for their rhetorical potential.

To structure this discussion, I first describe how accessibility has long been positioned only in terms of functional accommodations to digital texts—as a set of practices that help students overcome their issues in accessing pedagogical environments and texts. I reframe this discussion of overcoming as one of *coming over* in order to emphasize the importance of accessibility within multimodal frameworks as integral to teaching student writers how to become ethical producers of multimodal texts. I present examples from my own multimodal writing classrooms to illustrate how accessibility can be foregrounded, rather than treated as a retrofit or afterthought: from in-class activities to homework to major assignments. Accessibility is integral to learning, composing, and teaching, and I hope to emphasize the possibilities for disabled student writers to move and be in the classroom in ways that are true to their needs, knowledges, and literacies.

ACCESSIBILITY AS ETHICAL, RHETORICAL PRACTICE

In her oft-cited 1999 essay, "Technology and Literacy: A Story about the Perils of Not Paying Attention," Cynthia Selfe argues that rhetoric and writing instructors must take responsibility for both the technologies we use for our scholarship and those we require students to use in the classroom, because many students—specifically, students of color and low-income students—may lack access to these technologies. I want to make clear that taking responsibility for the technologies we use in the writing classroom also means ensuring the accessibility of these technologies and the texts students compose. Accessibility cannot be ignored if rhetoric and writing instructors want to engage with and teach responsible and ethical composing practices. In "Multimodality in Motion: Disability and Kairotic Spaces," M. Remi Yergeau and their colleagues call for more accessible multimodal pedagogies, arguing, "For educators, it is ethically questionable to practice pedagogies and construct spaces that categorically exclude entire classes of people."

An *ethics of accessibility*, the authors note, accounts for the material needs of both disabled students and instructors while also recognizing the need for writing curricula to be responsible and respectful of difference. This ethic connects both to classroom practices—such as lesson planning, assignment design, and the literacies and rhetorical practices that we privilege—and to disciplinary scholarship. Guaranteeing an ethics of accessibility, or creating a "culture of access" (Brewer et al.), involves a radical shift away from making accessibility decisions based solely on formal diagnoses and treating accommodations as retrofits that disabled student writers must use to overcome; instead, we need to create spaces where students have multiple access points for engaging content and expressing themselves—making space for students to *come over* to discussions of pedagogical accessibility.

In the classroom, accessibility is often only discussed or enacted as an accommodation to preexisting technologies and practices, rather than as a practice central to multimodal composing. This articulation imagines accessibility only as a retrofit—an added component to an already-built space. Retrofitting occurs beyond physical spaces, too. For example, if someone composes and publishes a podcast and it is pointed out to the creator that the podcast is inaccessible to deaf or hard-of-hearing users, the creator might produce a transcript that can be accessed with the podcast—retrofitting the original text with an accessible component. Stephanie Kerschbaum refers to this phenomenon as "multimodal inhospitality," which "occurs when the design and production of multimodal texts and environments persistently ignore access except as a retrofit" (Yergeau et al., "Multimodality"). M. Remi Yergeau teases out the connection between accommodations and retrofitting for accessibility, stating, "To accommodate is to retrofit; it is to assume normative bodies as default and to build spaces and infrastructures around those normative default bodies; it is to deal with deviant bodily and spatial conditions as they bubble out at the seams" (Yergeau et al., "Multimodality"). The production of inaccessible texts reproduces ableist assumptions about the normative default bodies that we imagine as our audiences, and the process of retrofitting these inaccessible texts does nothing to improve or engage systemic cultures of access that inform the composition and production of digital texts.

When accessibility is positioned as accommodation, it becomes merely a functional, institutional requirement rather than an opportunity to critically reflect on systemic practices. In *Multiliteracies for a Digital Age*, Stuart Selber critiques the simplification of a functional literacy that positions computers as a "means to an end" (36), arguing that there are clear problems with the tool metaphor: "Tools are accommodating in that they get integrated into a culture in ways that do not challenge its dominant belief systems" (38). This echoes critiques of institutional accommodations because, although accommodations are institutionally mandated, they do not significantly change institutional structures. Rather, accommodations exist as afterthoughts, legal requirements that "are predicated on problemed bodies and spaces rather than problemed infrastructures and practices" (Yergeau et al., "Multimodality"). Students and instructors in need of accommodation are responsible for securing their accommodations and, thus, inclusion into academic culture. Accommodations become ways to "fit in" to the mainstream (Jung 162), where overcoming and conforming to a normative ideal is the ultimate goal, rather than challenging oppressive structures that only grant accessibility based on individual disability diagnoses.

Just as we need understandings of accessibility that move beyond retrofitting and placing the blame within individual student bodies, so do we need more complex understandings of rhetorical expression and what literacies we value in the writing classroom. Functional literacy is often branded as a fixed skill that must be mastered and measured, but Selber argues for greater complexity and a bridging of critical and functional literacies: "Students need both functional and critical literacies (as well as other types of literacies like the rhetorical and visual literacies involved in Web site design and production)" ("Reimagining" 472). Specifically, Selber contends that functional literacy, "which offers certain kinds of *important access to a culture*" (497, emphasis added), must be reimagined and articulated *with* other literacies, rather than positioned in opposition to them—an approach that is more attentive to how functional operations exist within larger, systemic structures. This is an important reminder, too, to recognize the functional value of accommodations while, simultaneously, recognizing that accommodations *on their own* are not enough. I want to suggest that accessible practices can be functional *and* rhetorical, engaging students and encouraging them to critically interrogate how power circulates within digital contexts (Selber, *Multiliteracies* 133) and to become empowered producers of media who must self-consciously and self-critically make informed rhetorical decisions (160).

Accessibility is embodied, dynamic, and full of rhetorical potential. As multimodal and digital modes become increasingly common in the writing classroom, instructors must move away from treating accessibility as afterthought, retrofit, or accommodation, and instead position it as a central component of discussions of rhetoric and writing. Accessible practices—like transcripts, captions, and image descriptions—are often treated as functional accommodations that help students overcome the disabilities that prevent them from accessing a text. Accessible practices are opportunities not simply to accommodate texts but to encourage students to explore the rhetorical potential of accessibility: making ethical choices about how they represent content, voices, and sounds, and thinking critically about how those choices affect their audience.

And, while I do want to emphasize the rhetorical potential of accessible practices, such practices are also important for guaranteeing accessibility in ways that resist rhetorics of overcoming by removing barriers for disabled student writers and making space for the multiple ways students access, engage, and compose texts. In the rest of this chapter, I address practices that are usually regarded as accommodations rather than opportunities to create multiple access points for all students, in order to illustrate accessibility as a vehicle for empowering disabled student writers and making space for nonnormative expressions of rhetoricity within the multimodal writing classroom.

TRANSCRIPTION: MAKING SOUND ACCESSIBLE

Audio allows composers opportunities to create aural texts that experiment with voice, sounds, and music; to incorporate multiple voices to emphasize dialogue; and to convey moods and tones that traditional, print-based academic writing cannot. As Heidi McKee notes in "Sound Matters: Notes toward the Analysis and Design of Sound in Multimodal Webtexts," we are immersed in sound and it is a critical communicative mode, yet instructors tend to privilege visual design when teaching multimodal assignments, even though students' final products usually include sound (336). Excluding sound from discussions about composing multimodal texts prevents critical discussions about the accessibility of sound. In addition to encouraging students to attend to visual rhetorical choices, we need to give sound the same careful attention so as not to render a text inaccessible by relying too heavily on one mode.

In this section, I address transcription as a common example of an accommodating practice that people often consider only in terms of functional accessibility—positioning it as an afterthought or a stripped-down version of audio content. However, I illustrate how transcription functions rhetorically through both in-class activities and multimodal assignments. I focus first on podcasts, as they are arguably the most common audio-based writing assignment and, increasingly, a popular genre for circulating disciplinary knowledge in alternative formats. With the prevalence of podcasting within first-year writing program curricula, guaranteeing the accessibility of podcasts—and any assignment that relies on a single mode—is paramount. In addition to podcasts, I discuss a transcription assignment that I designed for a class on writing as information design, presenting it as one example of how to foreground accessibility in multimodal writing classrooms.

As a hearing person, I find podcasts inaccessible. Although I worked on the writing studies podcast *This Rhetorical Life* for three years as a doctoral student, I never listen to podcasts because I have a difficult time processing auditory information.[27] This is why I am immensely grateful at conferences when presenters offer full-text copies or even handouts of their presentations, and is also why I often live-tweet at conferences to focus my attention. Making audio accessible is important for deaf and hard-of-hearing audiences, and it can also be useful for people who do not or cannot focus on or process audio well, people who are in a time crunch (for whom skimming a transcript is often more effective), and people with unstable internet connections or limited data, who may benefit more from viewing a PDF than streaming audio. In addition to guaranteeing accessibility for users, transcription benefits student writers by allowing them to make creative, critical, and rhetorical choices.

Podcasting allows students to experiment with recording and editing, to frame an issue and make it *sound* interesting—through vocal delivery, music, and special effects—and to make rhetorical and creative choices about whose voices and what types of audio to include to enhance the final product. Computers and writing scholars have contributed greatly to scholarship about the potentials of using podcasts in the classroom (Bowie, "Podcasting" and "Rhetorical"; Cushman and Kelly; Dangler et al.; Jones; Krause; Reid; Zdenek, "Accessible Podcasting"). And writing center scholars have also contributed insights on the pedagogical potentials of podcasts (Cosby and Thompson; Lape; McKinney; Vee et al.). Although podcasts have been of interest to scholars of computers and writing for over a decade, there has been limited work that foregrounds or discusses transcription as anything other than a functional necessity or accommodating feature of an aural text. It is not my intent to argue for the value of incorporating podcasts in a writing classroom, although they are useful for generating discussions about genre, invention, audience, and rhetorical production. Rather, I contend that if instructors ask students to compose texts that involve audio, they must also emphasize considerations of accessibility in producing these texts.

Podcasts are accessible in the sense that they are readily available for people to download or stream, but are not necessarily accessible in terms of users easily or equally accessing their content. In "Accessible Podcasting," Sean Zdenek notes that access in podcast discourse is commonly equated with availability and *acquisition* of a podcast episode, but accessibility—making full use of the podcast itself—is left unattended. As Zdenek points out, "a podcast that is easy to use and readily available is not one that is, strictly speaking, accessible to people with disabilities" who may benefit from transcripts, text descriptions, or captions. Many tools are available that allow users, even those without much recording or podcasting experience, to immediately record and publish podcasts. With this immediate, do-it-yourself appeal, taking time to transcribe is not often part of the process. However, as Jennifer Bowie notes in "Podcasting in a Writing Class? Considering the Possibilities," requiring students to submit transcripts with their podcasts is important for nonhearing audiences or low-vision or blind individuals who use screen readers or other accessibility software. And in terms of time considerations, Bowie argues, "Usually students write out transcripts before they start recording the more formal assignments anyway, so it is often little extra work for them to submit these along with podcasts." At the least, then, students often already have a script that they can develop into a more detailed transcript.

Perhaps the general inaccessibility of podcasts as single-mode texts can be attributed to ableist assumptions that undergird a range of new media projects. Ableism, as defined by Fiona Kumari Campbell, is a "network of beliefs, processes and practices that produces a particular kind of self and body (the corporeal standard) that is projected as the perfect, species-typical and therefore essential and fully human" (44). Often, there are assumptions not only about who consumes media (e.g., a hearing audience) but also who composes the media (e.g., hearing students).[28] Ableism surfaces through the assumption that podcast users not only are hearing but also will access that audio the same way, resulting in a genre that often addresses an ideal, standardized body. Ableism often positions disabled people as fundamentally different from nondisabled populations (Mollow and McRuer 22). Imagining transcripts only through the lens of accommodations reinforces them as something *different* that benefits only a few, a mindset that does nothing to address the core issue of inaccessibility and instead perpetuates rhetorics of overcoming. Addressing ableist assumptions is the first step in engaging more inclusive conversations about accessibility as integral to new media and multimodal projects.

Rather than treating transcription separately, positioning it as part of multimodal composing—a process of making choices about what content is included and excluded—shifts the purpose from an accommodation to a rhetorical and creative act. Transcription allows us to critically examine the audio elements that we observe and value and those we tend to ignore. For example, fillers and silence are not typically elements that are included in a bare-bones transcript intended only to indicate verbal data. However, "relegating 'fillers' to secondary status or omitting them altogether deletes valuable information from a transcript" (Gilewicz and Thonus 28). The same is true for silence. As Cheryl Glenn has argued, not all silences have rhetorical meaning, but silence is too often dismissed as passive rather than as a "tactical strategy" (xi). Even though the delivery of silence is always the same, "the function of specific acts, states, phenomena of silence—that is, the interpretation by and effect upon other people—varies according to the social-rhetorical context in which it occurs" (9). The indication of silence as *[pause]* may look the same across transcripts but can have significantly different discursive meaning. In the podcast episode that I discuss next, literacy studies scholar Elaine Richardson's pauses are filled with many types of meaning. The silence of thinking differs greatly from her long pauses when she reflects on the violence against Black folks. Transcribing *only* to communicate dialogue silences these nonverbal "fillers," and approaching transcription rhetorically allows for representation of both textual and embodied communication.

There are multiple ways to incorporate transcription into the writing classroom, from playing a brief audio clip in class to introduce students to different audio elements, to giving homework assignments that ask students to transcribe audio and compare rhetorical choices with their peers, to developing assignments that ask students to collaboratively transcribe an audio file and reflect on the rhetorical choices they have made regarding speech and nonspeech sounds (e.g., music background noise, tone and pitch, emotion, silence, and the overall "mood" of the text). These could function as a series of scaffolded activities, but they could also be used individually, depending on the course context and goals. In a first-year writing course, for example, the first activity could jump-start discussions about rhetorical choices and the representation of certain sounds and information. In a course focused on the production of digital texts, a combination of these activities could be used to discuss rhetorical choices, emphasizing specific sounds and information, ethically representing voice, and translating content and meaning across media. A graduate course might emphasize more of the collaborative nature of multimodal texts and question what it means to produce accessible and ethical scholarship.

For example, I designed an in-class activity for a composition pedagogy graduate class using the first two minutes of a *This Rhetorical Life* podcast episode, "A One-Woman Show with Elaine Richardson," in order to prompt a discussion about ethical production and stylistic choices. After playing the clip twice, I asked folks to share what they noticed, using questions like, *What did you observe as relevant or important? What was left out? Did you try just to represent dialogue, or did you also note tones and background noises?* Everyone noted standard elements, such as words and dialogue and who was speaking. Most students also used italics, capital letters, and asterisks to indicate shifts in tone. Perhaps more surprising—or less standard—were suggestions about how to indicate temporal shifts of voices layered on top of each other, which prompted a discussion of the challenges of translating content across different media.

When asked what was left out of their observations, one student remarked that she was unsure whether she should represent the Black Vernacular English present in the clip. I chose this clip because it is playful and performative; because it involves multiple audio elements, including long pauses, snaps, and hands hitting the table; and because Elaine Richardson and interviewer Seth Davis dip in and out of Black Vernacular English. The question of whether to represent these language practices demonstrates the rhetorical potential and ethical dimensions of transcription. For example, we discussed the different ways to represent *rollin/rollin'/rolling*. *Rollin'* creates the illusion that something is missing and, thus, implies it is not the proper word, whereas *rolling* is the "standard" representation of the word but is not the word Elaine Richardson uses. We discussed audience (*How would different audiences read this representation of voice?*), the politics of representing voices that are not our own (*Is this accurate or ethical representation?*), and rhetorical considerations about style.

This clip ("A One-Woman Show" 0:35–01:12) is complex despite its brevity. I offer an excerpt from the episode's official transcript to illustrate how I chose to represent this audio:

> SD: We had a chance to sit and chat about the George Zimmerman trial, the memoir itself, African American rhetoric, and even RuPaul.
> SD: [*Chatter*] What was I going to say? I guess we can get, get st—
> ER: [*Chatter*] We gon make it happen.
> SD: [*Chatter*] Yeah, we gon make it happen. It'll be all right.
> ER: [*Singing*] Make it happen.
> SD: [*Chatter*] So is it recording?
> ER: [*Singing*] [*claps*] I know life can be so tough [*snaps*] and you feel like [*snaps*] givin up. [*Directed to Seth*] You remember that? [*Singing*] But you must be strong. [*claps*] Baby, [*snaps*] just hold on.

SD: Okay, here's my first question. This is easy. *From PHD to PhD*—
ER: Oh! So we goin? We rollin?
SD: We been goin!
ER: [*Screams*] Oh noooo!
SD: We been goin.
ER: Oh no! This is the real beginning. [*laughs*]

After practicing transcription,[29] many students noted the challenge of trying to represent certain sounds through text: snaps, claps, filler sounds, the emphasis of specific words, screams, time lapses, singing and background noise, tonal shifts, and even editing glitches. This activity took about thirty minutes from start to finish, and highlighted the multiple factors involved in making a text truly accessible. This is not to say that this much effort *must* go into transcribing; rather, I designed this activity to emphasize the combination of functional, creative, and rhetorical choices that inform an action that is most commonly viewed as nothing more than a chore. By discussing audience, ethical production, and stylistic choices, and situating them within larger contexts of meaning-making, accessibility becomes not a fixed, technical practice, but rather a dynamic rhetorical process.

In addition to an in-class activity, transcription can be a valuable out-of-class assignment in a multimodal writing classroom. For example, the last time I taught writing as information design—an upper-division professional writing course—I designed an audio transcription assignment, which I framed in terms of both genre and accessibility:

> We choose different genres for our communications based on the rhetorical situation, e.g., purpose, audience, context. For example, a newsworthy event may appear in a print newspaper, in an online article with links to resources, as part of a podcast episode, or as a video produced by the news organization or taken with a cell phone. Content and meaning are constantly translated and adapted across different media.

For the second project, we will discuss the genre affordances and constraints of audio and written text and (mis) representing content across different modes. We will also discuss composing accessible and ethical media and what it means to represent audio in ways that all people can access it. More specifically, you will transcribe five minutes of audio and reflect on the process of communicating content through different modes.

I asked students to include the audio clip or a link to the audio they transcribed, a typed transcript, and a two-page reflection about the rhetorical choices they made and what they learned about transcription through this process. The following example is a brief excerpt from a student's transcript from the 2015 film *Batman vs. Robin*:

> BW: Bruce Wayne (billionaire, Batman)
> SV: Samantha Vanaver (Bruce's romantic interest)
> DW: Damian Wayne (Bruce's son, Robin)
>
> DW: *[groans, yawns]* I was reading. I must have fallen asleep. What's . . . what's going on?
> SV: Oh, and who might this be?
> DW: I'm Damian, Bruce's -
> BW: - my ward. Well, he will be. Soon.
> SV: That's twice you've surprised me tonight.
> BW: Damian's had a difficult life and I don't want those vultures in the press corps descending on him just yet. So we've been -
> DW: *[bitterly]* - keeping me a secret.
> BW: Only until the paperwork is finalized. Then we'll proudly announce the newest addition to our family.
> BW: I should have told you, Samantha, but -
> SV: - no, there's nothing to apologize for. You've taken this unfortunate child and given him a chance at a better life. You have to do it your way. I respect that.
> *Cell phone chirps.*

There are a number of elements represented within these few seconds of video: dialogue to represent what is spoken, who is speaking at different times, overlapping speech, nonspeech sounds such as yawning, tonal shifts to indicate mood, and nonhuman sounds. In their reflection, the student wrote, "The biggest challenge is re-listening and re-listening to determine that the dialogue is correct. After the dialogue is correct, then the challenge is deciding what words should be stressed—if any—or if the tone of the voice should be conveyed." Dialogue is the most functional element and, often, this is as complex as transcription gets. Another student reported a similar experience:

> During the transcription process, I focused first on what each character said, and then on the context of each line to determine the tone and meaning, as well as the pacing of the scenes in the video. From there, I added parenthesis when necessary to explain further any misconceptions that could arise when reading the transcript.

As I've mentioned, dedicating an entire assignment to transcription is not the only way to foreground transcribing as a rhetorical practice; however, it was a useful way both to discuss genre and representing content across different modalities, and to ask a group of largely nondisabled students to consider a mode of communication—sound—in ways that they had not done before. This was a valuable assignment for discussing accessibility as integral to rhetorical decisions about audience and context, and as central to the composing process of multimodal texts. I chose the example of the *Batman vs. Robin* transcript not just because it was a thoughtful textual representation of audio content, but also because the student chose a film, rather than an audio file. In their reflection, they noted the difficulty of relying solely on transcription—rather than captioning or video description—to accurately and ethically communicate the meaning of the text.

CAPTIONING: MAKING VIDEO ACCESSIBLE

In 2010, YouTube made it possible for all user-generated content to have captions, using voice-recognition software (Ellis and Kent

139–40). In 2012, Netflix settled a class-action lawsuit filed by the National Association of the Deaf by agreeing to caption all of its shows by 2014, resulting in a payment of $755,000 in legal fees (Mullin). Despite this progress, closed captioning still runs the risk of poor, inconsistent regulation, even on mainstream platforms like Netflix: "By and large, closed captions on Netflix's instant streaming service are loaded with nonsense characters, transcription errors, and dialogue so implausible that it's hard to believe they're actually transcription errors. Many obscure the opening credits, line up poorly with spoken lines, or linger into uncomfortable stretches of silence" (Christian). Although Netflix agreed to caption its content, questions remain on the quality of the captions. Captioning is treated as a functional requirement, an afterthought, a retrofit with significant financial repercussions. Closed captioning is a prime example of an accommodating technology, because it has not historically been available from the beginning; rather, it became widespread in broadcast television *after* it was regulated by law, and we now face similar issues with online captioning. Ellis and Kent argue that "there comes a point where 'lack of awareness' can no longer be a viable excuse, particularly when accessibility measures are already available but simply not used for any justifiable reason" (139). I often see instructors overwhelmed by their lack of personal knowledge or awareness of accessibility, and when establishing an ethics of accessibility in the classroom, it's important for instructors to seek out information about captioning—and to collaborate with students and even the Office of Disability Services to learn more.

Just as transcription is necessary for making audio accessible, captioning is an integral practice for enabling the accessibility of visuals—specifically, videos and images. Like podcasts, video projects are common forms of the translation project (or remediation assignment) in first-year writing curricula, and instructors must attend to the accessibility of translation projects.[30] Students are often drawn to composing videos when digital projects are assigned, perhaps because of their familiarity with video-based social media apps and the ease of recording and editing on smartphones. Despite this familiarity, the prevalence of remediation projects, and an increasing number of tools available to caption videos, they remain widely inaccessible.

Captions, like transcripts, benefit deaf users and folks who have technological constraints or who may benefit from receiving the content both textually and orally. Brenda Brueggemann also observes that captioning video can help reach broader and more diverse audiences, making that video "instantly global" ("Articulating"). For example, captions can be very useful for English learners, allowing them to both hear and read the words. In this section, I address how captioning is important not simply as an accessible teaching practice, but also as a way to engage students in rhetorical and ethical discussions of purpose, audience, and context. Specifically, I discuss rhetorical elements that are specific to captioning, such as spatial constraints and visual rhetorical considerations, ultimately arguing that captioning is a practice that overcomes the inaccessibility of many multimodal texts. To support this claim, I present two examples: one video from a first-year writing class that uses text strategically to contextualize and make claims, and one video from an upper-division cultural rhetorics class that uses captions rhetorically to add another layer of meaning-making to the visual, audio, and embodied communication present in the video.

Creating captions is similar to composing transcripts in terms of making rhetorical choices about what content to include and how to represent it, but there are some significant differences. For example, when a podcast or aural text is retrofitted with a transcript, the final product is physically no different than if the composer had created a transcript from the start, because these are two separate documents. With a video, however, a transcript would exist outside of the multimodal text, and captions could be seamlessly incorporated into multimodal texts and experienced together with it. In this case, it would also be useful to have a transcript with video descriptions for blind and low-vision users.

In "Articulating Betweenity: Literacy, Language, Identity, and Technology in the Deaf/Hard-of-Hearing Collection," Brueggemann argues for privileging nonnormative literacy practices in order to create more robust texts, and she calls for a conceptualization of captioning as "a skill that we can apply our creative liberty to." Integral to this argument is the concept of *betweenity*, the construction of an identity that toggles, for example, between deaf and hearing or personal and academic. To be between is to exist relationally—constructing an idea, text, or oneself in relation to something or someone else. Captioning, for example, is made up of relational layers between text and speech, written and visual elements, the captioner and the audience. Although captioning is a tool for making video and film more inclusive, it is also a rhetorical practice. Describing the practices of her son, who captions her videos, Brueggemann writes, "Karl notes that he has learned to be attentive to the various extralinguistic (sublinguistic?) elements that accompany speech. Spoken words are, he suggests, mere words and there is so much more that comes along with communication and 'language' that a captioner might consider." She highlights the discursive potential of captioning, arguing that "meaning gets *made* through captioning as well." Captions toggle between text and speech and a range of audiences, and captioners must consider how best to make meaning through captioning.

Unlike transcription, captioning involves spatial constraints that add an extra element for rhetorical consideration. In "Which Sounds Are Significant? Towards a Rhetoric of Closed Captioning," Sean Zdenek lays important groundwork for thinking rhetorically about how captioning can enrich videos and contribute to the discursive meaning of a text, which necessarily involves making decisions about not only *how* to caption but also *what* to caption. "Caption space is limited," he notes. "Only significant sounds should be captioned" (Zdenek, "Which"). Certainly, significance is both subjective and interpretative, which makes it rhetorical but also tricky to navigate, which is why instructors should engage students in discussions about determining the significance of sounds, from dialogue to nonverbal utterances and embodied communications. In *Reading Sounds: Closed-Captioned Media and Popular Culture,* Zdenek writes, "The question of *significance* cuts to the heart of a rhetorical approach to captioning. Definitions of captioning often make a distinction, sometimes implicit, between significant and insignificant sounds. But they seem to assume that the question of *significance, importance,* or *essence* is a straightforward one, easily answered" (60). The captioner is responsible for captioning both sounds and the context that the audience needs to understand the narrative. Asking students to consider how to represent significant information within constrained spaces is a valuable way to improve understanding of rhetorical considerations of purpose, audience, and context.

Another critical rhetorical element that is unique to captioning is design—both visual rhetorical design and digital design. Although formatting may factor into transcribing, transcripts exist as documents separate from aural texts. Captions are integrated into the videos themselves, and because videos already rely heavily on visual elements, it is useful to consider the visual rhetoric of captions: how typeface, font size and color, and placement can affect the tone or meaning of the text. Students in my classes have used traditional white captions at the bottom of the screen, but students have also experimented with different sans serif fonts and colors (like yellow) and placement on the screen. Of course, these stylistic choices should still maintain accessibility, in terms of high contrast, readable text. Unlike transcribing, captioning also offers an opportunity to introduce another element of digital editing into students' digital composing processes.

I want to reimagine captioning as an organic element in the multimodal composing process that has rhetorical potential and discursive value. Many writing instructors already encourage students to use text in videos to tell a story along with the images, and we should engage students in conversations about ethical design. Captioning, though perhaps a new practice to both students and instructors, is necessary for assignments that require students to make meaning through a combination of modalities. Indeed, Janine Butler argues, "If we can appreciate that embodied captions can benefit deaf *and* hearing viewers and if we can move beyond seeing captions as accommodations, then we will have overcome the boundaries between modes of communication" ("Embodied"). Rather than creating multimodal texts that deny access to deaf viewers, the production of videos requires deaf students and users to *overcome* the pedagogical barrier. Making videos accessible means attending to the embodied, rhetorical potentials of captions.

As with transcription, there are a number of ways to incorporate captioning into the multimodal writing classroom. An in-class activity might ask students to watch a brief video clip with closed captioning and write down observations about the effectiveness of the captions and what sounds they deemed significant. A more advanced incorporation could be a homework assignment that asks students to watch a familiar show or movie, reflect on the rhetorical choices of the closed captions, and then share those thoughts in class. And, I contend, a multimodal assignment with a video component should require students to practice user-generated captioning. The goals of these scaffolded captioning practices are similar to those of the transcription assignments mentioned in the previous section: to introduce captioning as a rhetorical practice, make creative stylistic choices, consider what content is captioned, and prioritize the ethical production of video. These activities also create opportunities to engage students in discussions of visual rhetoric and digital design. Though there are many small-scale activities that could incorporate captioning, I want to offer two examples. The first is an assignment that is prominent in first-year writing curricula: the remediation assignment or translation project.

In most multimodal writing curricula, the remediation assignment functions as a translation of students' researched academic arguments into a multimodal text. Students identify a new audience, choose an appropriate medium for addressing that audience, and consider what elements of their research can be incorporated into this new multimodal text. The project also requires students to reflect on the rhetorical choices they have made about their medium, audience, and rhetorical appeals. When I started teaching my first-year writing classes focused on disability, mental health, and self-care, I began to highlight accessibility as part of the composing process—from using plain language to composing multimodal texts. I did so through class activities that asked students to engage in different embodied composing processes, and more explicitly through the language I used in assignment prompts for multimodal projects, as well as evaluation criteria:

Accessibility. The writer made the translation accessible to diverse audiences: videos are captioned, images are textually described, PowerPoints include scripts, audio is accompanied by a transcript, etc.

Accessibility must be part of assignment design. And, like the other elements that writing instructors assess, accessibility cannot simply be a matter of whether there *is* an accessible component, but whether that component actually meets the needs of a wide range of disabled audiences. Incorporating accessibility into assignment prompts and evaluation criteria signals to students that these elements are as valuable as making claims, organizing ideas, and selecting appropriate media and design elements.

In the spirit of Shipka's mediated activity-based multimodal framework that "requires students to assume responsibility for determining the purposes, potentials, and contexts of their work" ("Including" 88), the translation project asks students to determine their own media, audiences, and arguments. To account for the wide range of media that students use, I fold collaborative accessibility practices into in-class activities. For example, I create a "Tips and Tricks" Google Doc that everyone can edit, and then ask students to spend time finding a few useful resources to share, such as useful tutorials or best practices. In class, I group students based on their final project ideas and ask them to share the tips they learned about their media, compiling all the best practices into one cumulative resource. Within those groups, they do "accessibility brainstorms," where I prompt them to think about accessibility before they start drafting their projects. When issues of accessibility are highlighted at the forefront of a new multimodal project, ideally, students do less retrofitting.

The following example is a first-year writing student's translation project of the research they conducted about the stigma facing disabled parents in the United States. While they cited peer-reviewed sources and some primary sources that reported parents' specific experiences, the student chose to find clips of parents sharing their experiences on YouTube, and relied on these more than academic sources to make a statement about letting disabled folks speak for themselves. This involved some toggling (as Brueggemann would say) between audio, sound, and text, and the student used text in two ways: to make a claim and to caption dialogue. Here, I offer two examples that illustrate how my student used text discursively to construct their claim (see Figures 1 and 2).

I share this not as a groundbreaking use of text but as a common example of how we already encourage students to think about text within video composition to contextualize issues and make claims. A few of the YouTube clips of disabled parents discussing their experiences and challenges already had captioned dialogue, and the student added captions for spoken dialogue to the clips that lacked them. Capturing spoken dialogue is not the most rhetorically complex use of captions, but this student made rhetorical choices about how much text to include in each shot to emphasize specific words and ideas, and they applied different fonts to distinguish their ideas (represented through a large, black sans serif) from dialogue (repre-

6.1 million children in the United States have parents with disabilities...

Figure 1. Establishing exigency. This screenshot reads, "6.1 million children in the United States have parents with disabilities . . ." in large black font against a white background.

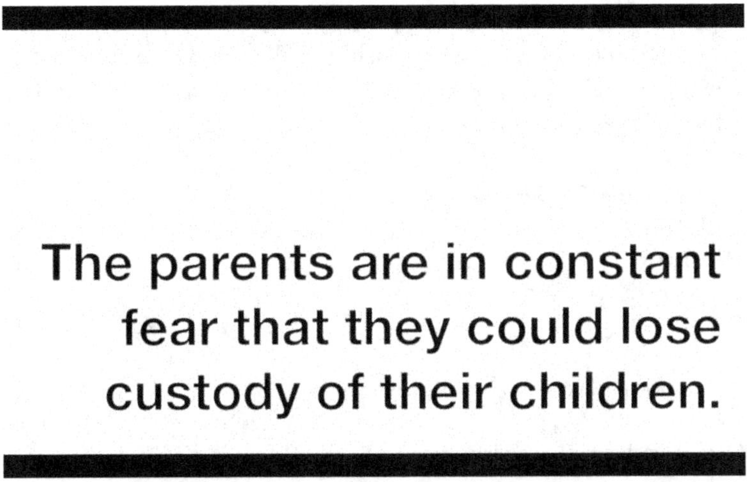

The parents are in constant fear that they could lose custody of their children.

Figure 2. Following exigency with a claim. This screenshot reads, "The parents are in constant fear that they could lose custody of their children" in large black font against a white background.

sented through a white sans serif with rounded letters). Rhetorical choices about accessibility could be foregrounded by developing a multimodal assignment focused on how captions function as another layer of text that adds meaning and creates access.

The second video I briefly highlight moves closer to the idea of captions as additional layers of meaning-making that add value in addition to supplementing the video. This second example is from an upper-division writing class where students were asked to compose their own cultural rhetorics stories using any combination of modes and materials they chose. To tell this story, my student created a series of three brief skits representing different elements of the rhetorics of coming out, and each video was accompanied by a brief narrative reflecting on the experience. I share this example as a more sophisticated form of captioning that involved a process of creative rhetorical choices that added another layer of meaning to the multimodal text. The videos and accompanying essays are focused on how marginalized folks are seen as *different* after disclosing in ways that feel intrusive, and captioning here becomes a way to take agency within the discussion and build on embodied experiences to demonstrate rhetoricity through a different form of media. While I present a screenshot in Figure 3, I offer the following textual representation of the captions to avoid including a screenshot for each still.

"Questioning People" Video (0:32)
[Male Friend]   [Female Friend]
Hey, have you seen To Wong Fu?
I've heard it's a great movie.

                                      Oh yeah! My girlfriend and I went to go see that.

Your girlfriend? Like *girlfriend* girlfriend?

                                      Yeah.

Okay! How long have you been together?

                                      Like 3 years.

That's so cool! Oh my gosh!
Is her family supportive? Is your family supportive? Are you guys gonna get married soon? Do you split your bills?
Who does the grocery shopping? I bet you share clothes! That's so cool, oh my gosh! Your closet, I'm sure you guys share it all . . .

Figure 3. Series of questions. This screenshot shows the captions for the final series of questions. The male friend sits on the left side of a couch, pointing at his friend, who sits on the right side of the couch and is avoiding eye contact with him. Everything is in black and white.

Following a brief, casual back-and-forth between two friends, one of the friends launches into a series of personal questions after learning his friend is queer and has a girlfriend. Unlike the textual representation of the dialogue presented on the previous page, in which brief captions are positioned underneath each character's name through the use of alignment (captions for the male friend are left-aligned, and captions for the female friend are right-aligned), in the video, the series of questions spans the width of the screen. She stands up and leaves the room as he asks his eighth question. So, what do these placement choices contribute to the overall narrative of the video?

In the written reflection accompanying this video, my student discussed the challenge that queer folks face when nonqueer people perceive such disclosures as an invitation to open their lives for questioning. When friends ask why she hasn't disclosed before, she said she tells them, "It is because of the pandora's box of questions that I may be susceptible to once I disclose my personal information." This reflection on being met with intrusive questions after coming out and disclosing personal information is represented not only in the scripted text of this video but also in the stylistic caption choices. In the first half of the video, the captions beneath each character are well within the bounds of each person's space, and there is equal back-and-forth of dialogue. The personal questions take over the rest of the video, and the captions reach across boundaries into the physical space of the female character who just disclosed. Here, the captioner (my student) toggles between short and long captions to mirror the process of navigating disclosure and the question of how much information to share—and, conversely, how much information needs to be asked. This is an example of the discursive potential of captions as nonnormative rhetorical expression. Captions themselves are not understood as a standard form of rhetorical expression; however, these captions contribute additional meaning to the spoken words and embodied communication of the two friends. They create a visual, textual argument about the constant questioning that queer people face when they come out in different contexts.

Captioning serves both functional and rhetorical purposes: preserving spoken dialogue while also representing important context that is indicated beyond words. And, while it may seem excessive to spend additional time in the classroom on captioning when platforms like YouTube have automatic captions built into their interfaces, I offer two counterarguments: First, automatic captions operate as functional accommodations that typically represent *most* of the information accurately but are riddled with mistakes, which reinforces accessibility as simply an afterthought.[31] Second, asking students to compose their own captions requires them to interact with media at a more intimate level, making rhetorical choices about what information to include and what the ethical consequences are of excluding or misrepresenting content. Captioning overlaps with the composing considerations that students already engage with when producing multimodal texts: concerns related to readability, design, and visual impact. I hope that these examples also highlight the importance of thinking of captioning not simply as a functional practice *or* a rhetorical practice, but instead imagining it as a complex practice that combines functional and rhetorical considerations to fulfill the purposes and needs of both the composer and audience.

ALT TEXT AND IMAGE DESCRIPTIONS: MAKING IMAGES ACCESSIBLE

Increasingly present in mainstream conversations about accessibility are alternative text (alt text) and image descriptions. Alt text is what screen readers read to blind and low-vision users to describe an image on a page, instead of simply saying "image." For a long time, alt text was only a conversation among web developers—a requirement of the Web Content Accessibility Guidelines (WCAG) 2.0 developed by the World Wide Web Consortium (W3C). More recently, alt text has been integrated into a number of mainstream interfaces, beginning with self-publishing platforms like WordPress and extending to social media platforms like Twitter, Facebook, and Instagram. Writing alt text—like the other accessible practices I have discussed in this chapter—is a rhetorical process. To illustrate this, I share an example from a student's digital collage on the rhetorical dimensions of silence. Another practice for making visual content accessible is the use of image descriptions, which I discuss both as a creative practice that allows marginalized students to express their nonnormative rhetoricity, and as a demonstration of the rhetorical potential of an accommodation. I share an example from Alice Wong, disability rights activist and host of the *Disability Visibility* podcast, to demonstrate how image descriptions are imagined within disabled communities, rather than tech industries. Finally, I end with an example from a student project that moves far beyond image description as a functional necessity and instead incorporates it as another modality for expressing meaning.

Before discussing alt text as creative expression, it is necessary to be familiar with its purpose and technical guidelines, which require more subjective choices than captioning dialogue. In *A Web for Everyone: Designing Accessible User Experiences*, Sarah Horton and Whitney Quesenbery argue that writing useful alt text is about communicating equivalent meaning: "To do this well, you have to think about the purpose of the image and its context of use, including whether there is information in the image that is not repeated elsewhere in the content. When alt text is too long, or has more information than is really meaningful, it can be distracting instead of adding to the experience" (155). Writing alt text involves making choices about what information is significant, similar to Zdenek's arguments about captioning. When writing alt text, it is important to include words that appear on the image; to ignore decorative or repetitive elements, such as icons and bullets; to move beyond simply repeating the file name; and to describe images in *meaningful* ways (Horton and Quesenbery 155–57). It can be tempting to think that more is better, but if alt text or image descriptions include information that is unnecessary for understanding the *content* and *context* of the image, then they do not truly meet audiences' needs.[32]

I offer one example here from a student's multimodal definition of rhetoric from an upper-division cultural rhetorics course. The student was influenced by discussions throughout the semester about communities whose rhetorical practices are silenced, and they used a quote from Tim Dougherty's article "Knowing (Y)Our

Story: Practicing Decolonial Rhetorical History" to frame the message of their digital collage: "We know that even our silence is a rhetorical act, and that it speaks volumes about where someone stands." The collage included a range of female protesters, from recognizable figures to unnamed protesters of different ages, ethnicities, and international locations. The collage also includes the poem "Silence Speaks Louder Than Words" by Girl.in.the.Rain. Because the design was created using text boxes in InDesign, all the text on the screen is accessible. Each of the seven images on the collage also has detailed alt text. Rather than showing every instance of alt text, I offer a cropped version of the collage that focuses on two images in Figure 4.

Each piece of alt text describes relevant text, what is pictured, and details about context, such as the empty speech clouds and the fact that these three women are supported by a group behind them. Arguably, this is a more advanced version of alt text than the automatically generated alt text in Microsoft Word: "A group of people around each other." The alt text written by this student contains concise yet detailed descriptions of both the content and context of the images selected to make a claim about the rhetoricity of silence.

Unlike alt text, which requires a program or device to reveal the text, an image description is usually formatted as a caption or in the post for all to see. Thus, while I teach alt text in classes where students engage in web development, I incorporate image descriptions into nearly all of my multimodal writing classes as an example of a universally designed, accessible—rather than accommodating—practice. There are multiple Instagram accounts that I use to teach image descriptions, including @disability_visibility and @national parkservice. I start with @disability_visibility, run by disability activist and media maker Alice Wong, as an example of how image descriptions are written by someone who is celebrated for her work and commitment to accessibility and disability justice. Here's a straightforward example from May 9, 2019: "Image Description: Graphic with a white background with a red border and black text that reads: Why is access, solidarity, and disability justice a practice of love? At the bottom, centered: #AccessIsLove" (@disability_visibility, "Access"). This offers a brief description of the visual context

Guaranteeing Access(ibility) in the Multimodal Writing Classroom / 113

Figure 4. Alt text for a digital collage. This is a zoomed-in version of a digital collage featuring only two of the seven included images and their corresponding alt text information. The images are stacked vertically. The alt text for the image at the top reads, "In part of a crowd, the focus is on three South African woman with black duct tape over their mouths, wearing matching purple T-shirts that read, 'SEXUAL VIOLENCE = SILENCE.'" The alt text for the image below reads, "Print artwork from Samanta Tello. Women of different ethnicities are pictured with only hair, lips, and some accessories. Beige speech clouds come from each woman's mouth, but each cloud is empty."

of the image and then transcribes the text. A more complex version is the image description for the cover image of Wong's podcast, *Disability Visibility*, which must necessarily be more detailed, not because there's more text (there isn't), but because personal branding is so important for sharing and trying to engage your work. It is also more complex because of Wong's commitment to representing herself the way she wants, her desire to extend thanks to the artist who created the illustration, and her description of the overall mix of visuals and text:

> Image description: Graphic with a bright yellow background. At the top in black text: "Disability Visibility". In the center: illustration by artist Mike Mort featuring an Asian American woman with black hair, red lips, and red headphones over her head. She is wearing a Bi-Pap mask that covers her nose and attached to a gray tube. She is also wearing a pair of purple sunglasses Below in black text: "Politics Culture Media, Hosted by Alice Wong" with a red dot between "politics" and "culture" and one between "culture" and "media." (@disability_invisibility, "disability_visibility")

Disability Visibility addresses and includes a wide range of disabled embodiments and disability rights issues, and especially in this context it makes sense to offer an image description that goes beyond simple accommodation to accessibly communicate equivalent meaning (note that I am not sharing the image itself) while allowing the host to represent herself in a way that's as true to herself as possible, even as an illustration. In the caption of the post and the image description, she amplifies the work of the disabled artist who designed the cover image—nodding to the collaborative work of accessibility and providing support to other folks in the disability community. Finally, this podcast is a form of art dedicated to interviewing and sharing space with other artists and activists, and, within this cultural and political context, the image description becomes not just an accessible offering but also a creative narrative of what the podcast is and how disability will be addressed.

I don't want to generalize too broadly from one example, but Alice Wong is certainly a good example of a disability rights activist dedicated to accessibility who removes barriers of overcoming in the media she circulates on social media so that folks with multiple access needs have immediate access to the content. I like to balance this example with that of an account with a much different purpose and style: @nationalparkservice. The National Park Service Instagram account is a nice example of a national organization prioritizing accessibility, because they write detailed captions and include a concise image description for each image they post. Their image descriptions are sometimes playful but always include the name of the animal(s) or scenery depicted and the name of the national park, which is important context for this particular account as they highlight specific parks in order to encourage people to visit them. For example, "Sun streaming across the forested landscape of Shenandoah National Park" describes a photograph of the sun setting (or perhaps rising) behind mountains covered in trees. There could be more detail here about color or time of day, but the description offers both content and context.

Image descriptions have become an integral part of my multimodal classrooms as I increasingly incorporate infographics, whether as a requirement (for example, in information design classes) or as an option for other multimodal projects. The push to transform texts into infographics, including course syllabi, is a great way to engage students multimodally, but infographics are often highly inaccessible documents. The proliferation of free platforms like Piktochart and Canvas allow folks to produce well-designed infographics without much web or design experience, so there is increased *access* to producing this form of knowledge, yet *accessibility* issues arise because these platforms allow users to save their documents only as flat image files. Discussion of how to write meaningful image descriptions for infographics and other complex technical images—and rhetorical choices about how to textually describe visual design choices—must be folded into class discussions about multimodal composing.

As one final example, I discuss an infographic that one of my students made on Canvas, highlighting one brief part of the student's accompanying transcript with image descriptions, as well as their reflection on their accessibility process. For this project, my student designed an infographic defining rhetoric, and one element of this was the claim that rhetoric is embodied. After reading *Techne: Queer Meditations on Writing the Self* by Jacqueline Rhodes and Jonathan Alexander, the student was struck by Rhodes's discussion of rhizomes. I offer both a screenshot from the visual text (Figure 5) and the transcript (formatting intact) describing the image (Figure 6).

While the placement of text and different forms of emphasis—such as boldface, italics, and capitalization—are not mirrored in the infographic and transcript, there are creative choices in both. And, while the choices differ, both texts indicate differences between elements (e.g., the text is written in a different font and color in the transcript). The transcript provides accessibility, but the student has also made creative choices about the rhetorical expression of this content. In their reflection, the student writes:

> To make the text accessible, I used a high-contrast, color-blind-accessible color palette and readable fonts. Infographics are not accessible to screen readers and similar software, so I included a transcript with detailed image descriptions instead of embedding these descriptions into the original text that a screen reader would not have been able to detect. While writing the transcript, I used the "Styles" option in Word for headers, subheaders, and body text because I learned in a Professional Writing class that this allowed for screen reader accessibility.

Often, accessibility is considered as one-dimensional—captions for a video, a written description of visual content—but this reflection points to the necessity of providing multiple access points when creating multimodal texts. This infographic is accessible to a range of disabled embodiments, and the richness of the transcript does more than remove technical barriers: it also demonstrates a focus on providing good experiences for everyone and designing texts that are *delightful* to use (Horton and Quesenbery 175). The student focuses both on textual and design choices with creative type choices, spacing, and alignment—expressing rhetoricity within a genre that is not often valued as real writing.

RHETORIC = EMBODIED

JACKIE RHODES

It is an ethical feminist move to come out... We pay for (in)visibility when we seek to contain or erase our multiple spaces, identities, affiliations. Here: I am a woman and I am a feminist and I am lesbian and I am queer and I am a rape survivor and I am a cutter and I am white.

Rhodes' multiple embodied identities exist both together and separately; influencing one another, but remaining their own. Each of these identities is rhetorical. **Rhetoric is not an abstract concept, but a part of us.**

Figure 5. Visual representation of infographic. The image description and text for this image are detailed in Figure 6. The infographic has a minimal color palette, with dark-purple backgrounds for titles and a white background for the main text. The image of the author is cropped into a circle, with the quote to the right of the image.

RHETORIC = EMBODIED

JACKIE RHODES [image: Author Jackie Rhodes smiles at the camera, her arms crossed]

It is an ethical feminist move to come out... We pay for (in)visibility when we seek to contain or erase our multiple spaces, identities, affiliations. Here: I am a woman and I am a feminist and I am lesbian and I am queer and I am a rape survivor and I am a cutter and I am white.

Rhodes' multiple embodied identities exist both together and separately; influencing one another, but remaining their own. Each of these identities is rhetorical. *Rhetoric is not an abstract concept, but a part of us.*

Figure 6. Student transcription of infographic.

As I've mentioned throughout these chapters, there is no one-size-fits-all solution to accessibility, and some transcripts may be more complex than others, depending on their context. The detail of the infographic transcript is necessary because this text-heavy multimodal project was designed in an easy-to-use interface that is ultimately inaccessible. For example, another student created an infographic for the same project using InDesign, which meant the text was scannable and they were able to create alt text. Many of the easily available visual interfaces are not accessible, at least not in their free versions, which are their major appeal for classroom use. Paying for an account allows users to save their infographics and visuals as PDFs, which would make the text readable but would still lack alt text. It is simply not feasible in all classes to assign work in a program like InDesign, but this software provides more control of accessibility with user-generated content and design, and could be useful to include in upper-division multimodal writing classes. There are a range of approaches to composing accessible multimodal texts, which is why the rhetorical nature of writing image descriptions, transcripts, captions, and alt text must be central to discussions of multimodal composing. Without these practices, we remain stuck in a process of asking students to create inaccessible texts and building more barriers that disabled viewers must overcome to access that content—whether it is a short creative video on YouTube or a scholarly multimodal webtext.

FOREGROUNDING ACCESSIBLE MULTIMODAL PRACTICES

Multimodal design must be accessible, inclusive design. Transcripts, captions, alt text, and image descriptions are all important practices for making digital texts accessible, but—as I have argued throughout *Rhetorics of Overcoming*—defining and teaching multimodal texts only as digital texts gives some students new composing options while simultaneously denying access to others, and it is possible to create an agentive rhetorical classroom without reliance on digital texts. As a final example, then, I want to highlight a nondigital multimodal text from a recent cultural rhetorics course. I assigned a multimodal definition of rhetoric as the final project, asking students to define their understandings of rhetoric based on the semester's readings and discussions, and, because of the role inclusion played throughout the semester, I wrote this requirement specifically into the assignment:

Access and inclusion are two important themes from this semester: Who has access to rhetorical theory and history? How can the field be more inclusive to different bodies, minds, knowledges, and experiences? It is vital that your multimodal text is accessible. Videos must be captioned, images must be described, audio must be transcribed, etc.

While many of these projects were digital in nature—such as videos, infographics, visual essays, and websites—many were not. I also received zines, collages, and paintings. There are a number of nondigital multimodal examples that I could reference, and I've discussed some of these in Chapter 2, but here I want to briefly address one student's process of making their abstract painting accessible through the use of both image descriptions and braille.

The canvas was filled with black triangles that transformed into multicolored circles as they traveled from the bottom-left corner to the top-right, and horizontal lines of braille ran across the bottom of the canvas—reproduced using nail polish to re-create the tactile experience of raised dots. The triangles symbolized Aristotle's definition of rhetoric, and their transformation into different shapes and colors symbolized the cultural forms of meaning-making that have been excluded from traditional definitions. The braille itself communicated the student's definition of rhetoric, serving a purpose beyond its functional value as an accommodating component of a visual text. The student used braille to add semantic meaning to the piece, and the braille text was, arguably, the most descriptive part of the piece—articulating the ideas symbolized by the shapes. It's important to note here that incorporating braille into this piece was not what made it accessible, and the painting was accompanied by a textual image description. The braille—typically an accommodating component—was not treated as a technical component, but was instead foregrounded as the core communicative element of the project. A blind user who could read braille would not need to overcome the inaccessibility of this visual text by accessing a retrofitted component; instead, the sighted user must overcome their inability to read braille and access the image description to understand the full meaning of the piece.

I want to be clear: accessibility must be discussed throughout the composition process, rather than isolated to a single "day of access" that addresses the ethics of producing digital texts. Folding accessible practices into writing curricula highlights the importance of accessibility, as well as the ways in which considering accessibility makes students more rhetorically adept. Accessibility in this context cannot simply be a note in the assignment prompt that transcripts are required; rather, accessibility needs to be foregrounded in both the design of assignments and class discussions about aural composing. Accessibility is a practice that moves beyond functional necessity or legal requirement, and foregrounding the ethical and rhetorical dimensions of accessibility is a necessary step for guaranteeing that students both have access to texts and compose texts that are accessible to a wide range of people. Instructors must also consider how to model accessibility in the classroom. For example, I try to model what I want from students: offering print handouts, posting class notes, captioning any videos that I use or create, and describing slides when I present lectures.

Finally, I have not intended to disparage the necessity of accommodations; rather, I hope to have demonstrated how accessible practices like transcribing and captioning have traditionally been positioned *only* as functional accommodations—as practices that help students overcome their difficulties in accessing a text. Throughout this chapter, I have argued for a shift from accommodation to accessibility. Institutional accommodations are frequently positioned as afterthoughts and individual measures that address problems at a micro level without addressing larger systems of inaccessibility. Enacting an ethics of accessibility challenges the notion that instructors can meet disabled student writers' needs only if those students have been formally diagnosed and present appropriate documentation at the beginning of the semester. By incorporating theories of accessibility in the classroom, instructors can foreground discussions of the discursive potentials of accessibility as a rhetorical practice. How people access texts is necessarily influenced by embodied, affective processes of meaning-making, and there must be room for these processes in the multimodal writing classroom. Simply put, teaching students to create multimodal texts without attending to accessibility is unethical, limits students' understandings of audience and meaning-making, and results in the production of potentially interesting but ultimately inaccessible information.

5

Conclusion: Toward an Ethics of Accessibility

I BEGAN THIS BOOK WITH A series of disclosures. For me, these disclosures are a way to make clear my own positionality in taking on this work, an acknowledgment of how disability and accessibility cannot be separated from my experiences within higher education, first as a student and now as a professor. Disclosure is a rhetorical negotiation, a complex and ongoing process, and—as is often the case in spaces of higher education—an asymmetrical power dynamic when disclosure is necessary for guaranteeing equitable treatment. As I have noted, disclosure can be weaponized against both disabled students and disabled faculty, overtly through stigma and discrimination, subtly through microaggressions, and even unintentionally through the pedagogical action we take upon disclosure.

I have argued throughout *Rhetorics of Overcoming* that disclosure—along with diagnosis, accommodation, remediation, and cure/overcoming—is an integral component of rhetorics of overcoming. In the college writing classroom, rhetorics of overcoming manifest in desires to diagnose students or have students self-disclose disabilities, in pedagogies that position disability as an individual issue that should be addressed through accommodations rather than a rethinking of practices, in assumptions that disabled students' needs are so different from nondisabled students' needs that they *cannot* be addressed, and through scholarship that details diagnostic characteristics and prescribes practices based on those characteristics. I hope to have illustrated the many ways that demanding these disclosures further isolates disabled students and often results in accommodating practices that are static, remediative, and focused more on diagnostic criteria than students' material needs.

The process of accommodations demands individual disclosures in order to provide individualized accommodations, thus reinforcing the idea that accessibility is something that need not be taken up beyond an individual basis. This also reinforces the idea that disability is something that instructors do not need to consider in course design because, if someone cannot access or fully engage the material, they can simply request an accommodation. I have repeatedly argued that this absolves instructors of responsibility, positions disability *only* as something that must be cured rather than an embodiment that can transform our pedagogical practices, and forces students to share information that they should not have to share in order to obtain equitable treatment. As I have noted, there are a number of reasons why students do *not* disclose, from a lack of identification with disability identity, to a lack of access to diagnosis, to a fear of discrimination. If you think someone who has power over you is going to discriminate against you, infantilize you, or treat you *differently* because you have a disability—and you can sufficiently "hide" that disability—why would you disclose it?

Disclosure is a process of trust. I engage in a process of disclosures because I trust that speaking truthfully about my experiences as a mentally disabled academic is important for ensuring the ethical treatment of other academics. When students disclose to us, they trust us to take that information and do what is most appropriate to ensure their academic success and well-being. As a way to actively resist rhetorics of overcoming, I have proposed that we engage in the process of *coming over*—a collaborative process that embraces difference and emphasizes the agency of disabled students and faculty to overcome ableist pedagogical expectations by challenging systemic issues of physical and pedagogical inaccessibility. Engaging in coming over involves, in part, co-constructing writing spaces that are accessible to and inclusive of students with nonnormative rhetorical practices and a wide range of embodiments. I want to suggest that disclosure can be a useful part of this process because, while I have illustrated the complexities and problems of relying on students to self-disclose, I hope to have also shown the rhetorical potential of disclosure and the ways in which instructors, mentors, and administrators can take up students' disclosures in ways that are transformative rather than punitive, that move us away from simply providing *access* to reimagining *accessibility.*

As a field committed to social justice, alternative methods of composing and knowing, and meeting diverse students' needs, writing studies is in a critical moment to reimagine accessibility. While more writing teachers and scholars have recognized that disability and difference cannot be ignored, the task of responding to disability and building accessible infrastructures is more complex than advocating for any single practice or pedagogy for all students. Developing accessible pedagogies that resist rhetorics of overcoming requires collective action and a radical shift in how we understand disability and disabled student writers, both in pedagogical and research practices. This process begins with critical self-reflection, both programmatically and personally. It requires asking questions about how—and why—we privilege the knowledges, modes of communication, rhetorical expressions, and embodiments that we do.

Administrators of first-year writing programs, undergraduate and graduate programs, writing centers, and Writing Across the Curriculum initiatives must consider the following: What does success look like within your program? How is it assessed? How are students expected to demonstrate knowledge to earn their degrees? When does a challenging curriculum become an obstacle, and who might be *excluded* from the design of your major and minor, degree requirements, or exam processes?

Instructors should pause and reflect on their classroom practices: What does good writing look like? How is it assessed? What cultural and social barriers are in place in the classroom that prevent students from succeeding? Whose literacies are valued, both explicitly—written into the syllabus and assignment prompts, discussed and encouraged in class—and implicitly, and whose are denied or denigrated? What forms of engagement are encouraged or viewed as "unproductive"? Radically shifting from providing access *solely* through accommodations to building more accessible infrastructures begins with questioning and acknowledging personal, programmatic, and disciplinary assumptions about disability and disabled student writers.

I have focused primarily on how rhetorics of overcoming manifest in writing spaces, but, as I noted at the outset of this book, this problem is not unique to writing studies. Resisting rhetorics of overcoming also involves recognizing the ways in which these discourses manifest beyond the classroom, within the day-to-day activities of the university, and asking questions about how we can work across disciplines to actively rewrite medicalized narratives of disability, disabled students, and accessibility. I invite you to look critically at your own university environments: What are the structures and rhetorics of overcoming that manifest in your own university spaces, forcing disabled students, faculty, and staff to "overcome" their disabilities (by disclosing, pushing through, receiving retrofitted accommodations) in order to succeed in these academic environments? How can you work with people within your departments, colleges, and universities to resist these discourses and practices? And, perhaps more important, how can we build accessible infrastructures that are informed by disabled people's material needs, lived experiences, and embodied knowledges?

Throughout *Rhetorics of Overcoming,* I have explored multimodality and universal design as two frameworks that, taken together, present opportunities to develop more accessible learning and composing environments. In these final pages, I want to return to multimodality and UD not only to illustrate how they can be taken up beyond the classroom to guarantee access(ibility), but also to reiterate that implementation of a multimodal pedagogy does not ensure accessibility when it ignores disabled embodiments. I do this by offering two snapshots of university spaces: a committee meeting and a multimodal professional development event.

At a university committee meeting, I lean forward to look at the projector screen with the day's meeting agenda, locating the file in my inbox on my iPad. Beside me, there are a few physical handouts and materials that were also included in the email sent prior to the meeting. The slides for guest presentations have been provided in advance. Queenie sleeps curled in a ball at my feet under the conference room table. When someone speaks, their name is announced (thanks, *Robert's Rules of Order!*), which is an important accessibility move for blind folks to know who is speaking.

In many of the professional spaces I occupy on campus, this scene is quite common. While it may not have been set up specifically with multimodal accessibility or UD in mind, a meeting like this demonstrates several simple accessibility moves. Certainly, the goals of a meeting and a classroom are different (I imagine we can all agree that meetings are more efficient when everyone has access to the materials), but the accessible delivery of information—clear communication in multimodal modes so that everyone understands the content—is an important shared purpose. The question, for me, becomes, *Why don't these accessibility measures extend to classroom contexts?*

Flash forward two years, to when I decide to register for a weeklong professional development event about multimodal teaching and learning. I want to know how the university imagines the goals and design of multimodal pedagogy—especially as everyone scrambles to move mostly online (I'm finishing these final revisions in the midst of the global coronavirus pandemic). It's a solid curriculum focused on delivering material in multiple modes, crafting transparent assessment measures, and communicating with students in different ways. Each day offers readings, resources, and live webinars about multimodal teaching. We are assured from day one that the goal is accessibility. During a presentation about course design, a diagram of the principles of universal design for learning flashes across the screen, and the presenter notes the importance of following the principles—visualized on the screen but not described aloud—before moving on.

Of course, when we were told that the focus of the workshop— and of multimodal teaching more broadly—was accessibility, I assumed we would discuss disability accessibility. But in this case, as in many cases, *accessibility* really meant *access*. I requested captioned content when I registered for the event and received a reassuring email promising that all video content from the presenters would be captioned, but noting that the video examples made by former workshop participants would not. While the organizers have recognized the importance of accessibility in the delivery of their own content, they have not encouraged instructors to follow suit, and disability accessibility is not discussed throughout the week. Video production is a key focus of the week's curriculum as a method for engaging students multimodally, and I wait for the moment when we will discuss making those videos accessible. It doesn't come.

As I argued in the previous chapter, modeling accessibility is integral to disrupting the perpetuation of rhetorics of overcoming. That is, accessibility must be both modeled by instructors, administrators, and facilitators and taught to students, new faculty, and workshop participants. Otherwise, we will continue to produce—and encourage others to produce—texts and practices that are inaccessible.

I share these two snapshots of university spaces and events not to show why one is accessible and one is not, but to illustrate the complexities of multimodal accessibility and the (unintentional) harm that can be done when access is decoupled from considerations of embodiment. In her work on transformative justice, educator and organizer Mia Mingus points out that "you work to not only address the harm and the immediate needs the harm created, but you also make sure that the harm does not happen again and that you are working to transform the conditions that allowed the harm to happen in the first place." Ensuring accessibility is important, but just as important is transforming the systems that create inaccessibility. Individualized access—where texts and practices are retrofitted and accessibility takes place at the individual level—simply isn't enough to resist rhetorics of overcoming and create accessible pedagogical environments. As a field, I want us to move away from access for access's sake and toward an ethics of accessibility that prioritizes disability justice in our classroom and research spaces.

Shifting our focus to disability justice and developing an ethics of accessibility means actively working to show disabled students that we support them, value a wide range of embodied rhetorical practices, and prioritize access through course design and everyday practices. It necessarily involves collaboratively working with disabled students and faculty, rather than making decisions about accessibility that are based on isolated interactions with students or scholarship that generalizes disabled experiences. As the famed disability rights slogan states, "Nothing about us without us." A simple yet important step in creating a culture of accessibility is to have direct and honest conversations with each other, our students, and research participants about accessibility.

Many of us who do disability work have heard the reoccurring question, "I have a student with [this disability]. What would you do?" It's one of those well-intentioned questions from a teacher who really wants to make sure they meet their students' needs—especially in ways that are neither outdated nor offensive. I want to suggest that this is the wrong question. How might the answer change if it was reframed as a question for students: "What do you need?" I want to be clear, though, that inviting students to share their experiences does nothing to disrupt rhetorics of overcoming if we do not have a plan for what to do with this information:

> It is not enough to just make sure that we can get into the room or that the conversation is translated or that we can access the materials. And it is not enough for us to simply get to share what's important to us (though I know that many times we don't even get to share that), if no one knows how to hold what we are sharing; if no one knows how to understand and fully engage with what we are sharing. (Mingus)

As I have noted elsewhere, many folks respond to disclosures within the framework of disability as deficit, responding to disability characteristics rather than what a disclosure means for students' access needs. Disrupting this process means listening—really listening—to students' disclosures of what disability means to them. Asking disabled students to share their experiences and access needs cannot just be treated as one more step in a linear process of access that retrofits preexisting practices; rather, disabled embodiments are transformative to accessible pedagogy and must be treated as such.

Conclusion: Toward an Ethics of Accessibility

By mapping writing studies scholarship about disability, addressing how rhetorics of overcoming manifest in this scholarship and through different teaching and consulting practices, and reimagining accommodating practices as rhetorical and agentive, I have emphasized the value of centering accessibility rather than treating it as an afterthought or mere accommodation. I have argued that recognizing how rhetorics of overcoming inform our attitudes, assumptions, and interactions with disabled students is necessary for co-constructing more inclusive writing pedagogies and helping our students (and ourselves) become more ethical, socially just producers and consumers of texts. Pedagogical theories of multimodality and universal design are not solutions to rhetorics of overcoming, but I hope to have shown that their shared attention to multiple and embodied ways of knowing can usefully inform how we engage with disability, both in theory and in practice. Explicitly addressing disability and accessibility in conversations about literacy and writing in multiple modes foregrounds the role of accessibility in composing.

How students access and compose texts is necessarily influenced by embodied, affective processes of meaning-making, and we must make room for those processes in our writing pedagogies.

NOTES

1. The decision to use identity-first language rather than person-first is intentional, and the reasons are multiple. I use identity-first language in recognition that *disability* is not a bad word, aligning myself with folks who advocate for naming and valuing disability as an inherent way of being, navigating, and making meaning in the world (see Brown). It is also a linguistic decision. Instead of discussing students with disabilities as passive subjects, I hope to suggest that taking steps toward accessibility requires explicitly addressing disability and engaging with disabled student writers who know best about their experiences and needs. These decisions are intentional yet not universal, and I defer to the choices of individuals for how they choose to name and represent themselves.
2. As I argue in subsequent chapters, new media and multimodal practices can increase accessibility when incorporated consciously, but they are not inherently accessible.
3. To be clear, not all narratives of overcoming are negative. Wendy Harbour et al. draw attention to the ways in which overcoming has a history of pathologizing disability, but also of African American empowerment rooted in the Civil Rights Movement that "implies a community of individuals united against all odds" (155).
4. Breast cancer is not limited to cisgender women. While there is not a lot of research about transgender men and women in connection to breast cancer, hormone replacement therapy is associated with an increased risk of breast cancer. According to the National Center for Transgender Equality, the risk of breast cancer increases for trans women after five or more years of hormone therapy, and transgender men who have undergone top surgery are also at risk because not all breast tissue is removed (Kim).
5. According to Susan G. Komen's *Annual Report for Fiscal Year 2017 (Annual Report),* the organization's total assets from April 1, 2016, to March 31, 2017, were $347,909,642 (21).

6. In March 2014, the #NoMakeupSelfie campaign began as a movement in the United Kingdom to naturalize the beauty of women without makeup, but quickly became paired with raising money for cancer research. As Eliana Dockterman wrote in a *Time* article about the movement, "The pairing of the two seems to imply that taking a selfie without makeup compares in bravery in some way to battling cancer. It doesn't."
7. Disabled activists and disability studies scholars often use the reclaimed language of *crip* as a theoretical stance—akin to *queer*—that centers disability and reorients spaces and practices that are often designed to exclude disabled bodies. It is at once an identity, a verb, and a theoretical framework. Price and Kerschbaum use *crip* as a critical framework for restructuring the power dynamics within their qualitative research study. Others have discussed the possibilities of *crip* as a framework for reimagining first-year writing. For example, in *Crip Theory: Cultural Signs of Queerness and Disability*, McRuer argues that first-year writing demands standard writing produced by standard bodies within a system that upholds able-bodiedness as the norm. The result is a final "perfect" product that is so fetishized that the messy, embodied process cannot be acknowledged at all. McRuer asks us to reimagine composition, to *crip* it. Cripping composition involves imagining what exists beyond the standard forms of academic writing, making space for the bodies that do not fit these normative expectations, and valuing different embodied ways of learning and composing.
8. All study participants' names are pseudonyms.
9. Medical and social models are frequently pitted as opposites, but these models do not so easily exist in opposition, and these binary distinctions of medical/social and outsider/insider do not fully account for academic discourses, attitudes, or treatments of disability. This binary opposition has been troubled by feminist and critical disability studies scholars who have adopted *critical disability studies* as a way to move beyond the medical/social binary to account for lived experiences and the social, political, and economic dimensions of disability.
10. Kimber Barber-Fendley and Chris Hamel discuss the articles about LD published in English and composition journals between 1979 and 2004 in "A New Visibility: An Argument for Alternative Assistance Writing Programs for Students with Learning Disabilities," so I will not detail them here. I highlight a couple to provide an overview of the conversations about LD and how they reinforce and, in some cases, complicate the overcoming narrative.

11. Patricia Dunn also advocates for multisensory teaching strategies in *Learning Re-Abled: The Learning Disability Controversy and Composition Studies*. Dunn's text, published in 1995, predates many of the social model arguments about disability in writing studies, and Dunn makes visible the complexities of learning disability discourses and the challenges of LD student writers by tracing how LD has been addressed in our disciplinary scholarship, interviewing college students with LD about their experiences, and offering multisensory teaching strategies. She argues, "Incorporating multisensory options into regular coursework and assessment will expand educational opportunities for everyone and reveal talents that many students, LD or otherwise, may not have known they had" (201).
12. CAST's Universal Design for Learning Guidelines advise, "Unless specific media and materials are critical to the goal (e.g., learning to paint specifically with oils, learning to handwrite with calligraphy) it is important to provide alternative media for expression" ("UDL Guidelines").
13. UD and universal design for learning are two theories that emerged from different disciplines, and while one focuses on physical accessibility and the other on pedagogical accessibility, I use the term *universal design* throughout *Rhetorics of Overcoming*—although *universal design for learning* may be more accurate—because I'm centering the core principles of UD and physical, social, and pedagogical accessibility rather than breaking down and applying the corresponding guidelines for each theory.
14. The principles of UDL emerged in 2002 and were then developed into specific guidelines that educators can adapt and apply to different learning contexts, which some of the CAST researchers outline in their 2014 book *Universal Design for Learning: Theory and Practice*.
15. The ADA was passed in 1990, and the Individuals with Disabilities Education Act (IDEA) was renamed in 1990 (originally the Education of Handicapped Children Act of 1975).
16. This approach is similar to distinguishing LD students from the "mentally retarded, emotionally impaired, or grossly illiterate" (Richards 68) in early basic writing scholarship, as highlighted in Chapter 2.
17. Many have argued against the specialization of tutoring, contending instead that consultants have a broad range of rhetorical knowledge that they can apply to all sessions. Yet Moore et al. highlight the benefits of creating guides for assisting students with different learning styles, developing cheat sheets that help tutors identify par-

ticular LD characteristics and that offer practical strategies. They note that without the proper context, the guides would be overly simplistic: "Using the guides without prior training regarding the complexities of disability and culture, tutors could be tempted to use a 'one size fits all' approach with such students, an approach that for obvious reasons is ineffective" (5).

18. This example also points to a significant gap between K–12 and postsecondary education professional development. Whereas K–12 instructors are required to complete professional development related to disabled students, few college instructors are.
19. Although Hawkes contends that disabled students are savvy about their legal rights, this claim is in conflict with the low percentage of students who disclose disabilities and request accommodations (see Cortiella and Horowitz; Walters, "Toward"; Wood, *Disability*).
20. This echoes much of what Schmidt et al. report from their work with Casey, a deaf writing center student. Casey recommends that consultants "attempt to learn a few basic signs; become familiar with Deaf culture and the nuances of [American Sign Language] itself; allow for extended time when meeting with deaf student-writers, especially those who work with interpreters; and coordinate with the office of disability services to post schedules in the writing center that advertise interpreters' schedules of availability and contact numbers" (10).
21. LeAnn Nash also argues that we need greater cultural understanding of deaf students, because there are different subcultures and dialects even within Deaf culture—moving the conversation *away* from deafness as a rigid category.
22. Hawkes echoes this: "Offering a simple alternative of using a computer to make draft revisions versus requiring handwritten revisions will be an appreciated gesture" (374).
23. Factors such as a lack of resources, training, and expertise may make crafting accessible multimodal practices seem impossible. I discuss the potential of technologies to increase accessibility and meet students' needs in ways that more traditional practices have not, but it is not my goal to suggest that a focus on technology is the only way to increase accessibility. Rather, I argue that this moment is an opportunity to assess current pedagogical practices and craft more socially just writing center practices.
24. Broader conceptions of multimodality also acknowledge that not all writing center staff have access to the types of resources necessary to develop and sustain multiliteracy or multimodal pedagogies when those pedagogies are defined within the context of new media.

25. The 2017 edited collection *Writing Centers and Disability* makes a powerful statement about the value of disabled experiences in our disciplinary discourse by amplifying the voices of disabled student writers (Kitchens and Dukhie; Price, "Writing Up"), consultants (Babcock, "Interpreted"; Mucek; Weber), and administrators (Ellis).
26. Initially, I asked students to sign up for specific days at the beginning of the semester, but now I just mention collaborative note-taking throughout the semester, asking students to engage the notes in class to remind them that the document exists. I wrote about the logistics of this practice when I was a HASTAC (Humanities, Arts, Science, and Technology Alliance and Collaboratory) scholar: file:///Users/allisonhitt/Downloads/www.hastac.org/blogs/allisonhitt/2014/02/04/01-collaborative-note-taking.
27. I never perceived this as an issue until 2013, when I started working on a podcast intended to disseminate information relevant to writing studies instructors, scholars, and students. I don't mind not listening to trendy podcasts, but I often feel like I'm missing out on important academic knowledge. There are now over a dozen writing studies, rhetoric, and technical communication podcasts, and the majority do not have a visually accessible component. These podcasts both grant access to academic knowledge in a different and often timelier format, and deny access when disseminated in only one mode.
28. In "Multimodality in Motion," Sushil K. Oswal addresses ableist digital environments that affect both blind students and faculty, pointing to the importance of paying attention to accessibility for *everyone* in the classroom and at all levels of the composing process.
29. In most situations, transcribing would be a stressful and inaccessible activity to do in class—unless it was in a computer lab where students could use headphones and listen to the audio clip as many times as they needed to, but I wanted to illustrate the challenges of transcribing even just thirty-seven seconds of audio. When I've done this in subsequent classes, I have chosen no more than fifteen seconds.
30. In *Remixing Composition*, Jason Palmeri argues that we must recognize the limitations of alphabetic texts as the valued modality (46). His suggestion for this is the "translation project," sometimes referred to as a *remediation assignment*, where students translate a written essay into a multimedia presentation that often takes the form of a visual presentation, video, or infographic.

31. The YouTube channel "Rhett & Link: Caption Fails" is a great tool to use in class to demonstrate the limitations of functional accommodations such as automatic captions.
32. WebAIM provides a thorough discussion of how to write alt text ("Alternative Text"), and Anne-Marie Womack and her collaborators at Tulane University dedicate a page to image accessibility on their Kairos Award–winning website, Accessible Syllabus ("Image").

WORKS CITED

"About UDL." *UDL on Campus: Universal Design for Learning in Higher Education,* CAST, udloncampus.cast.org/page/udl_about. Accessed 5 Apr. 2021.

"About Us." *Pass It On,* The Foundation for a Better Life, www.passiton.com/who-we-are. Accessed 1 May 2019.

Alexander, Jonathan, and Jacqueline Rhodes. *On Multimodality: New Media in Composition Studies.* National Council of Teachers of English, 2014.

"Alternative Text." *WebAIM,* Center for Persons with Disabilities, Utah State University, 14 Oct. 2019, webaim.org/techniques/alttext/.

American Cancer Society. "Americans with Disabilities Act: Information for People Facing Cancer." 24 May 2016, www.cancer.org/treatment/finding-and-paying-for-treatment/understanding-financial-and-legal-matters/americans-with-disabilities-act.html.

Annual Report: Fiscal Year 2017. Susan G. Komen, 2017, www.komen.org/wp-content/uploads/2016-2017-Annual-Report.pdf. Accessed 1 July 2017.

Arola, Kristin L., and Anne Frances Wysocki, editors. *Composing (Media) = Composing (Embodiment): Bodies, Technologies, Writing, the Teaching of Writing.* Utah State UP, 2012.

Autism Speaks. "This story of overcoming the obstacles will make your night. #AutismAwareness." *Facebook,* 29 Nov. 2015, 6:30 p.m., www.facebook.com/autismspeaks/posts/10153753059007497. Accessed 1 Mar. 2017.

Babcock, Rebecca Day. "Disabilities in the Writing Center." *Praxis: A Writing Center Journal,* vol. 13, no. 1, 2015, www.praxisuwc.com/babcock-131/. Accessed 15 July 2017.

———. "Interpreted Writing Center Tutorials with College-Level Deaf Students." Babcock and Daniels, pp. 185–230.

———. *Tell Me How It Reads: Tutoring Deaf and Hearing Students in the Writing Center.* Gallaudet UP, 2012.

Babcock, Rebecca Day, and Sharifa Daniels, editors. *Writing Centers and Disability*. Fountainhead, 2017.

Barber-Fendley, Kimber, and Chris Hamel. "A New Visibility: An Argument for Alternative Assistance Writing Programs for Students with Learning Disabilities." *College Composition and Communication*, vol. 55, no. 3, Feb. 2004, pp. 504–35, doi:10.2307/4140697.

Berta, Renee. "Computer Modifications for Disabled Students." *The Writing Lab Newsletter*, vol. 14, no. 9, May 1990, pp. 6–7, wlnjournal.org/archives/v14/14-9.pdf.

Bérubé, Michael. "Pressing the Claim." Foreword. *Claiming Disability: Knowledge and Identity*, by Simi Linton, New York UP, 1998, pp. vii–xii.

Bowie, Jennifer L. "Podcasting in a Writing Class? Considering the Possibilities." *Kairos: A Journal of Rhetoric, Technology, and Pedagogy*, vol. 16, no. 2, Spring 2012, technorhetoric.net/16.2/praxis/bowie/. Accessed 15 July 2017.

———. "Rhetorical Roots and Media Future: How Podcasting Fits into the Computers and Writing Classroom." *Kairos: A Journal of Rhetoric, Technology, and Pedagogy*, vol. 16, no. 2, Spring 2012, technorhetoric.net/16.2/topoi/bowie/. Accessed 15 July 2017.

Boyle, Coleen A., et al. "Trends in the Prevalence of Developmental Disabilities in US Children, 1997–2008." *Pediatrics*, vol. 127, no. 6, 1 June 2011, pp. 1034–42, doi:10.1542/peds.2010-2989.

Breast Cancer Facts & Figures 2019-2020. American Cancer Society, 2019, https://www.cancer.org/content/dam/cancer-org/research/cancer-facts-and-statistics/breast-cancer-facts-and-figures/breast-cancer-facts-and-figures-2019-2020.pdf.

Brewer, Elizabeth, et al. "Creating a Culture of Access in Composition Studies." *Composition Studies*, vol. 42, no. 2, Fall 2014, pp. 151–54, www.uc.edu/content/dam/uc/journals/composition-studies/docs/WWA/Brewer%20Selfe%20Yergeau%2042.2.pdf.

Brown, Lydia X. Z. "The Significance of Semantics: Person-First Language: Why It Matters." *Autistic Hoya*, 4 Aug. 2011, www.autistichoya.com/2011/08/significance-of-semantics-person-first.html. Accessed 5 Apr. 2021.

Bruch, Patrick L. "Universality in Basic Writing: Connecting Multicultural Justice, Universal Instructional Design, and Classroom Practices." *Basic Writing e-Journal*, vol. 5, no. 1, Spring 2004, bwe.ccny.cuny.edu/Issue%205.1.html. Accessed 15 July 2017.

Brueggemann, Brenda Jo. "Articulating Betweenity: Literacy, Language, Identity, and Technology in the Deaf/Hard-of-Hearing Collection."

Stories That Speak to Us: Exhibits from the Digital Archive of Literacy Narratives, edited by H. Lewis Ulman et al., Computers and Composition Digital Press, 2013, ccdigitalpress.org/stories/brueggemann.html. Accessed 15 July 2017.

———. "Still-Life: Representations and Silences in the Participant-Observer Role." *Ethics and Representation in Qualitative Studies of Literacy*, edited by Peter Mortensen and Gesa E. Kirsch. National Council of Teachers of English, 1996, pp. 17–39.

Brueggemann, Brenda Jo, et al. "Becoming Visible: Lessons in Disability." *College Composition and Communication*, vol. 52, no. 3, Feb. 2001, pp. 368–98, doi:10.2307/358624.

Butler, Janine. "Embodied Captions in Multimodal Pedagogies." *Composition Forum*, vol. 39, Summer 2018, compositionforum.com/issue/39/captions.php. Accessed 1 Nov. 2018.

———. "Where Access Meets Multimodality: The Case of ASL Music Videos." *Kairos: A Journal of Rhetoric, Technology, and Pedagogy*, vol. 21, no. 1, Fall 2016, kairos.technorhetoric.net/21.1/topoi/butler/index.html. Accessed 15 July 2017.

Campbell, Fiona Kumari. "Inciting Legal Fictions: 'Disability's' Date with Ontology and the Ableist Body of Law." *Griffith Law Review*, vol. 10, no. 1, 2001, pp. 42–62.

"Cancer." *World Health Organization*, 3 Mar. 2021, www.who.int/newsroom/fact-sheets/detail/cancer. Accessed 5 Apr. 2021.

"CDC Estimates 1 in 68 Children Has Been Identified with Autism Spectrum Disorder." *Centers for Disease Control and Prevention*, 27 Mar. 2014, www.cdc.gov/media/releases/2014/p0327-autism-spectrum-disorder.html. Press release.

"CDC: 1 in 4 US Adults Live with a Disability." *Centers for Disease Control and Prevention*, 16 Aug. 2018, www.cdc.gov/media/releases/2018/p0816-disability.html. Press release.

Cedillo, Christina V. "What Does It Mean to Move?: Race, Disability, and Critical Embodiment Pedagogy." *Composition Forum*, vol. 39, Summer 2018, compositionforum.com/issue/39/to-move.php.

Center for Collegiate Mental Health (CCMH) 2015 Annual Report (Publication No. STA 15-108), Penn State, Jan. 2016, ccmh.psu.edu/assets/docs/2015_CCMH_Report_1-18-2015-yq3vik.pdf.

Center for Collegiate Mental Health (CCMH) 2018 Annual Report (Publication No. STA 19-180), Penn State, Jan. 2019, ccmh.psu.edu/assets/docs/2018-Annual-Report-9.27.19-FINAL.pdf.

Ceraso, Steph. "(Re)Educating the Senses: Multimodal Listening, Bodily Learning, and the Composition of Sonic Experiences." *College English*, vol. 77, no. 2, Nov. 2014, pp. 102–23.

———. *Sounding Composition: Multimodal Pedagogies for Embodied Listening*. U of Pittsburgh P, 2018.

Christian, Jon. "How Netflix Alienated and Insulted Its Deaf Subscribers." *The Week*, 30 Jan. 2014, theweek.com/articles/452181/how-netflix-alienated-insulted-deaf-subscribers.

Collins, Terry. "Helping Writers with Asperger's Syndrome." *The Writing Lab Newsletter*, vol. 32, no. 9, May 2008, pp. 14–15, wlnjournal.org/archives/v32/32.9.pdf.

Connor, David J., and Beth A. Ferri. "Historicizing Dis/Ability: Creating Normalcy, Containing Difference." *Foundations of Disability Studies*, edited by Matthew Wappett and Katrina Arndt, Palgrave Macmillan, 2013, pp. 29–68.

Corbett, Joan O'Toole. "Disclosing Our Relationships to Disabilities: An Invitation for Disability Studies Scholars." *Disability Studies Quarterly*, vol. 33, no. 2, 2013, dsq-sds.org/article/view/3708/3226. Accessed 1 July 2017.

Cortiella, Candace, and Sheldon H. Horowitz. *The State of Learning Disabilities: Facts, Trends and Emerging Issues*. 3rd ed., National Center for Learning Disabilities, 2014, www.ncld.org/wp-content/uploads/2014/11/2014-State-of-LD.pdf.

Cosby, Brooke, and Danielle Melissovas Thompson. "The Podcast Producers: A Guide to Really Useful Knowledge Podcasts." *The Writing Lab Newsletter*, vol. 34, no. 2, Oct. 2009, pp. 14–15, wlnjournal.org/archives/v34/34.2.pdf.

Crawford, Felicity A., and Lilia I. Bartolomé. "Labeling and Treating Linguistic Minority Students with Disabilities as Deficient and Outside the Normal Curve: A Pedagogy of Exclusion." *The Myth of the Normal Curve*, edited by Curt Dudley-Marling and Alex Gurn, Peter Lang, 2010, pp. 151–70.

Cushman, Jeremy, and Shannon Kelly. "Recasting Writing, Voicing Bodies: Podcasts Across a Writing Program." *Soundwriting Pedagogies*, edited by Courtney S. Danforth et al., Computers and Composition Digital Press / Utah State UP, 2018, ccdigitalpress.org/book/soundwriting/cushman-kelly/index.html.

Dangler, Doug, et al. "Expanding Composition Audiences with Podcasting." *Computers and Composition Online*, Spring 2007, cconlinejournal.org/podcasting/. Accessed 15 July 2017.

"Data and Statistics on Autism Spectrum Disorder." *Centers for Disease Control and Prevention*, 5 Apr. 2019, www.cdc.gov/ncbddd/autism/data.html. Accessed 1 May 2019.

Davidson, Cathy N. *Now You See It: How the Brain Science of Attention Will Transform the Way We Live, Work, and Learn*. Viking, 2011.

Degner, Hillary, et al. "Opening Closed Doors: A Rationale for Creating a Safe Space for Tutors Struggling with Mental Health Concerns or Illnesses." *Praxis: A Writing Center Journal*, vol. 13, no. 1, 2015, www.praxisuwc.com/degner-et-al-131. Accessed 15 July 2017.

@disability_visibility (Alice Wong). "Access Is Love." *Instagram*, 9 May 2019, www.instagram.com/p/BxPaRPxBb5K/.

———. "disability_visibility." *Instagram*, 11 Feb. 2019, https://www.instagram.com/p/BtxO-aFBNG0/.

Dockterman, Eliana. "#NoMakeupSelfie Brings Out the Worst of the Internet for a Good Cause." *Time*, 27 Mar. 2014, https://time.com/40506/nomakeupselfie-brings-out-the-worst-of-the-internet-for-a-good-cause/. Accessed 1 Mar. 2017.

Dolmage, Jay Timothy. *Academic Ableism: Disability and Higher Education*. U of Michigan P, 2017.

———. *Disability Rhetoric*. Syracuse UP, 2014.

———. "Mapping Composition: Inviting Disability in the Front Door." Lewiecki-Wilson and Brueggemann, pp. 14–27.

———. "Writing against Normal: Navigating a Corporeal Turn." Arola and Wysocki, pp. 110–26.

Dolmage, Jay, et al. "'I Simply Gave Up Trying to Present at CCCC . . .': A Conversation with the Committee on Disability Issues in College Composition." *Listening to Our Elders: Working and Writing for Change*, edited by Samantha Blackmon et al., New City Community Press / Utah State UP, 2011, pp. 56–86.

Dolmage, Jay, and Cynthia Lewiecki-Wilson. "Refiguring Rhetorica: Linking Feminist Rhetoric and Disability Studies." *Rhetorica in Motion: Feminist Rhetorical Methods and Methodologies*, edited by Eileen E. Schell and K.J. Rawson, U of Pittsburgh P, 2010, pp. 23–38.

Dunn, Patricia A. *Learning Re-Abled: The Learning Disability Controversy and Composition Studies*. Boynton/Cook, 1995.

Dunn, Patricia A., and Kathleen Dunn De Mers. "Reversing Notions of Disability and Accommodation: Embracing Universal Design in Writing Pedagogy and Web Space." *Kairos: A Journal of Rhetoric, Technology, and Pedagogy*, vol. 7, no. 1, Spring 2002, kairos.technorhetoric.net/7.1/binder2.html?coverweb/dunn_demers/. Accessed 15 July 2017.

Ellis, Carol. "Her Brain Works." Babcock and Daniels, pp. 31–45.

Ellis, Katie, and Mike Kent. *Disability and New Media*. Routledge, 2011.

Erevelles, Nirmala, et al. "How Does It Feel to Be a Problem? Race, Disability, and Exclusion in Educational Policy." *Who Benefits from Special*

Education? Remediating (Fixing) Other People's Children*, edited by Ellen A. Brantlinger, Routledge, 2008, pp. 77–100.
"Fast Facts: Students with Disabilities." *National Center for Education Statistics,* nces.ed.gov/fastfacts/display.asp?id=60. Accessed 5 Apr. 2021.
Ferri, Beth. "A Dialogue We've Yet to Have: Race and Disability Studies." *The Myth of the Normal Curve,* edited by Curt Dudley-Marling and Alex Gurn, Peter Lang, 2010, pp. 139–50.
Fishman, Teddi. "When It Isn't Even on the Page: Peer Consulting in Multimedia Environments." Sheridan and Inman, pp. 59–73.
Garland-Thomson, Rosemarie. "Integrating Disability, Transforming Feminist Theory." *Feminist Disability Studies,* edited by Kim Q. Hall, Indiana UP, 2011, pp. 13–47.
———. "The Politics of Staring: Visual Rhetorics of Disability in Popular Photography." *Disability Studies: Enabling the Humanities,* edited by Sharon L. Snyder et al. Modern Language Association of America, 2002, pp. 56–75.
Garrison, Kristen. "The Personal Is Rhetorical: War, Protest, and Peace in Breast Cancer Narratives." *Disability Studies Quarterly,* vol. 27, no. 4, Fall 2007, dsq-sds.org/article/view/52/52.
Gilewicz, Magdalena, and Terese Thonus. "Close Vertical Transcription in Writing Center Training and Research." *The Writing Center Journal,* vol. 24, no. 1, Fall/Winter 2003, pp. 25–49. *JSTOR,* www.jstor.org/stable/43442188.
Gleason, George. "A Reader Asks . . ." *The Writing Lab Newsletter,* vol. 9, no. 3, Nov. 1984, pp. 6–7, wlnjournal.org/archives/v9/9-3.pdf.
Glenn, Cheryl. *Unspoken: A Rhetoric of Silence.* Southern Illinois UP, 2004.
Grimm, Nancy Maloney. "Rearticulating the Work of the Writing Center." *College Composition and Communication,* vol. 47, no. 4, Dec. 1996, pp. 523–48. *JSTOR,* doi:10.2307/358600.
———. "Tutoring Dyslexic College Students: What These Students Teach Us about Literacy Development." *The Writing Teacher as Researcher: Essays in the Theory and Practice of Class-Based Research,* edited by Donald A. Daiker and Max Morenberg, Boynton/Cook, 1990, pp. 336–42.
Hamel, Christine M. "Learning Disabilities in the Writing Center: Challenging Our Perspectives?" *The Writing Lab Newsletter,* vol. 26, no. 8, Apr. 2002, pp. 1–5, wlnjournal.org/archives/v26/26.8.pdf.
Hamraie, Aimi. *Building Access: Universal Design and the Politics of Disability.* U of Minnesota P, 2017.
———. "Designing Collective Access: A Feminist Disability Theory of

Universal Design." *Disability Studies Quarterly*, vol. 33, no. 4, 2013, dsq-sds.org/article/view/3871/3411. Accessed 1 July 2017.

Harbour, Wendy S., et al. "'Overcoming' in Disability Studies and African American Culture." Kerschbaum et al., pp. 149–69.

Harris, Muriel. "Preparing to Sit at the Head Table: Maintaining Writing Center Viability in the Twenty-First Century." *The Writing Center Journal*, vol. 20, no. 2, Spring/Summer 2000, pp. 13–22. *JSTOR*, www.jstor.org/stable/43442095.

Hawkes, Lory. "When Compassion Isn't Enough: Providing Fair and Equivalent Access to Writing Help for Students with Disabilities." *The Writing Center Director's Resource Book*, edited by Christina Murphy and Byron L. Stay, Lawrence Erlbaum, 2006, pp. 371–78.

Hershey, Laura. "From Poster Child to Protester." *Independent Living Institute*, 1993, www.independentliving.org/docs4/hershey93.html. Accessed 1 July 2017.

Hewett, Beth L. "Helping Students with Learning Disabilities: Collaboration between Writing Centers and Special Services." *The Writing Lab Newsletter*, vol. 25, no. 3, Nov. 2000, pp. 1–5, wlnjournal.org/archives/v25/25.3.pdf.

Hitt, Allison H. "Making Space for Non-normative Expressions of Rhetoricity." *The Routledge Handbook of Digital Writing and Rhetoric*, edited by Jonathan Alexander and Jacqueline Rhodes, Routledge, 2018, pp. 175–85.

Horton, Sarah, and Whitney Quesenbery. *A Web for Everyone: Designing Accessible User Experiences*. Rosenfeld Media, 2013.

Hull, Glynda, and Mike Rose. "Rethinking Remediation: Toward a Social-Cognitive Understanding of Problematic Reading and Writing." *Written Communication*, vol. 6, no. 2, April 1989, pp. 139–54, doi:10.1177/0741088389006002001.

"Image." *Accessible Syllabus*, created by Anne-Marie Womack et al., www.accessiblesyllabus.com/image/. Accessed 15 Nov. 2019.

Inman, James A. "Designing Multiliteracy Centers: A Zoning Approach." Sheridan and Inman, pp. 19–32.

Jackson, Rebecca, and Jackie Grutsch McKinney. "Beyond Tutoring: Mapping the Invisible Landscape of Writing Center Work." *Praxis: A Writing Center Journal*, vol. 9, no. 1, 2011, www.praxisuwc.com/jackson-mckinney-91. Accessed 15 July 2017.

Jones, Leigh A. "Podcasting and Performativity: Multimodal Invention in an Advanced Writing Class." *Composition Studies*, vol. 38, no. 2, 2010, pp. 75–91.

Jung, Julie. "Textual Mainstreaming and Rhetorics of Accommodation." *Rhetoric Review*, vol. 26, no. 2, 2007, pp. 160–78, doi:10.1080/07350190709336707.

Kafer, Alison. *Feminist, Queer, Crip*. Indiana UP, 2013.

Kerschbaum, Stephanie L. "On Rhetorical Agency and Disclosing Disability in Academic Writing." *Rhetoric Review*, vol. 33, no. 1, 2014, pp. 55–71, doi:10.1080/07350198.2014.856730.

———. *Toward a New Rhetoric of Difference*. National Council of Teachers of English, 2014.

Kerschbaum, Stephanie L., et al., editors. *Negotiating Disability: Disclosure and Higher Education*. U of Michigan P, 2017.

Kiedaisch, Jean, and Sue Dinitz. "Changing Notions of Difference in the Writing Center: The Possibilities of Universal Design." *The Writing Center Journal*, vol. 27, no. 2, 2007, pp. 39–59. *JSTOR*, www.jstor.org/stable/43442271.

Kim, Mul K. "Transgender People and Breast Cancer." *National Center for Transgender Equality*, 29 Oct. 2010, transequality.org/blog/transgender-people-and-breast-cancer. Accessed 1 Mar. 2019.

Kitchens, Marshall W., and Sandra Dukhie. "Speech-to-Text: Peer Tutoring, Technology, and Students with Cognitive Impairments." Babcock and Daniels, pp. 163–84.

Konstant, Shoshana Beth. "Multi-sensory Tutoring for Multi-sensory Learners." *The Writing Lab Newsletter*, vol. 16, nos. 9–10, May–June 1992, pp. 6–8, wlnjournal.org/archives/v16/16-9-10.pdf.

Kopelson, Karen. "Risky Appeals: Recruiting to the Environmental Breast Cancer Movement in the Age of 'Pink Fatigue.'" *Rhetoric Society Quarterly*, vol. 43, no. 2, Apr. 2013, pp. 107–33, doi:10.1080/02773945.2013.768350.

Krause, Steven D. "Broadcast Composition: Using Audio Files and Podcasts in an Online Writing Course." *Computers and Composition Online*, Fall 2006, cconlinejournal.org/krause1/. Accessed 15 July 2017.

Kress, Gunther. "Multimodality." *Multiliteracies: Literacy Learning and the Design of Social Futures*, edited by Bill Cope and Mary Kalantzis, Routledge, 2000, pp. 179–99.

Lape, Noreen. "Giving Voice to Tutors' Really Useful Knowledge: A New Plan for Writing Center Podcasts." *The Writing Lab Newsletter*, vol. 34, no. 2, Oct. 2009, pp. 1–5, 13, wlnjournal.org/archives/v34/34.2.pdf.

Lefebvre, Henri. *The Production of Space*. Translated by Donald Nicholson-Smith, Blackwell, 1991.

Lewiecki-Wilson, Cynthia, and Brenda Jo Brueggemann, editors. *Disability and the Teaching of Writing: A Critical Sourcebook*. Bedford/St. Martin's, 2008.

Lewiecki-Wilson, Cynthia, and Brenda Jo Brueggemann. "Rethinking Practices and Pedagogy: Disability and the Teaching of Writing." Introduction. Lewiecki-Wilson and Brueggemann, pp. 1–9.

Linton, Simi. *Claiming Disability: Knowledge and Identity.* New York UP, 1998.

Mann, April. "Structure and Accommodation: Autism and the Writing Center." *Autism Spectrum Disorders in the College Composition Classroom*, edited by Val Gerstle and Lynda Walsh, Marquette UP, 2011, pp. 45–74.

McAlexander, Patricia J. "Using Principles of Universal Design in College Composition Courses." *Basic Writing e-Journal*, vol. 5, no. 1, Spring 2004, bwe.ccny.cuny.edu/Issue%205.1.html.

McHarg, Molly. "The Dual Citizenship of Disability." *The Writing Lab Newsletter*, vol. 36, nos. 7–8, March–April 2012, pp. 14–15, wlnjournal.org/archives/v36/36.7-8.pdf.

McKee, Heidi. "Sound Matters: Notes toward the Analysis and Design of Sound in Multimodal Webtexts." *Computers and Composition*, vol. 23, no. 3, 2006, pp. 335–54, doi:10.1016/j.compcom.2006.06.003.

McKinney, Jackie Grutsch. "New Media Matters: Tutoring in the Late Age of Print." *The Writing Center Journal*, vol. 29, no. 2, Fall 2009, pp. 28–51. *JSTOR*, www.jstor.org/stable/43460756.

McRuer, Robert. *Crip Theory: Cultural Signs of Queerness and Disability.* New York UP, 2006.

"Mental Health: A University Crisis." *The Guardian*, www.theguardian.com/education/series/mental-health-a-university-crisis. Accessed 1 July 2017.

Meyer, Craig A. "Disability and Accessibility: Is There an App for That?" *Computers and Composition Online*, Spring 2013, cconlinejournal.org/spring2013_special_issue/Meyer/. Accessed 15 July 2017.

Mingus, Mia. "'Disability Justice' Is Simply Another Term for Love." *Leaving Evidence,* 3 Nov. 2018, leavingevidence.wordpress.com/2018/11/03/disability-justice-is-simply-another-term-for-love/. Accessed 1 Mar. 2020.

Mollow, Anna, and Robert McRuer. Introduction. *Sex and Disability*, edited by Robert McRuer and Anna Mollow, Duke UP, 2012, pp. 1–36.

Moore, Julie L., et al. "Designing Tutor Guides to Enhance Effectiveness across Disciplines and with Special Demographics." *The Writing Lab Newsletter*, vol. 34, nos. 4–5, Dec. 2009–Jan. 2010, pp. 1–5, wlnjournal.org/archives/v34/34.4-5.pdf.

Mucek, Sarah A. "Identity and the Disabled Tutor: The Possibilities of Re-constructing Selfhood in Peer Writing Conferences." Babcock and Daniels, pp. 105–28.

Mullin, Joe. "Netflix Settles with Deaf-Rights Group, Agrees to Caption All Videos by 2014." *Ars Technica*, 10 Oct. 2012, arstechnica.com/tech-policy/2012/10/netflix-settles-with-deaf-rights-group-agrees-to-caption-all-videos-by-2014/. Accessed 1 July 2017.

Nash, LeAnn. "ESL in a Different Light: Can You Hear Me Now?" *The Writing Lab Newsletter*, vol. 32, no. 9, May 2008, pp. 1–5, wlnjournal.org/archives/v32/32.9.pdf.

@nationalparkservice (National Park Service). "Shenandoah National Park." *Instagram*, 7 May 2019, www.instagram.com/p/BxLjm95HPgq/.

Neff, Julie. "Learning Disabilities and the Writing Center." *The Longman Guide to Writing Center Theory and Practice*, edited by Robert W. Barnett and Jacob S. Blumner. Pearson, 2008, pp. 376–90.

New London Group. "A Pedagogy of Multiliteracies: Designing Social Futures." *Multiliteracies: Literacy Learning and the Design of Social Futures*, edited by Bill Cope and Mary Kalantzis, Routledge, 2000, pp. 9–37.

North, Stephen M. "The Idea of a Writing Center." *College English*, vol. 46, no. 5, Sept. 1984, pp. 433–46, doi:10.2307/377047.

Novotney, Amy. "Students under Pressure." *Monitor on Psychology*, vol. 45, no. 8, Sept. 2014, www.apa.org/monitor/2014/09/cover-pressure. Accessed 1 May 2019.

"A One-Woman Show with Elaine Richardson." *This Rhetorical Life*, episode 16, 4 Dec. 2013, thisrhetoricallife.syr.edu/episode-16-a-one-woman-show-with-elaine-richardson/. Accessed 15 July 2017.

"Overcaem Dyslexia." *Pass It On*, The Foundation for a Better Life, www.passiton.com/inspirational-sayings-billboards/20-hard-work. Accessed 1 May 2019.

Palmeri, Jason. *Remixing Composition: A History of Multimodal Writing Pedagogy*. Southern Illinois UP, 2012.

"Position Statement on Disability and Writing Centers." *International Writing Centers Association,* 2006, docs.google.com/document/d/1chDcrGHIiN-8NZgWKWsn5dFpJr9WK-GpArqg0IMejRg/edit.

Price, Margaret. "Accessing Disability: A Nondisabled Student Works the Hyphen." *College Composition and Communication*, vol. 59, no. 1, Sept. 2007, pp. 53–76. *JSTOR*, www.jstor.org/stable/20456981.

———. "Disability Studies Methodology: Explaining Ourselves to Ourselves." *Practicing Research in Writing Studies: Reflexive and Ethically Responsible Research*, edited by Katrina M. Powell and Pamela Takayoshi, Hampton Press, 2012, pp. 159–86.

———. *Mad at School: Rhetorics of Mental Disability and Academic Life.* U of Michigan P, 2011.

———. "Writing Up the Academy: A Disabled Student and Her Tutor Negotiate the English Major." Babcock and Daniels, pp. 129–60.

Price, Margaret, et al. "Disclosure of Mental Disability by College and University Faculty: The Negotiation of Accommodations, Supports, and Barriers." *Disability Studies Quarterly*, vol. 37, no. 2, Spring 2017, dsq-sds.org/article/view/5487/4653.

Price, Margaret, and Stephanie L. Kerschbaum. "Stories of Methodology: Interviewing Sideways, Crooked and Crip." *Canadian Journal of Disability Studies*, vol. 5, no. 3, 2016, doi:10.15353/cjds.v5i3.295.

Pryal, Katie Rose Guest. *Life of the Mind Interrupted: Essays on Mental Health and Disability in Higher Education.* Blue Crow Publishing, 2017.

"Quadriplegic. A-. Harvard." *Pass It On*, The Foundation for a Better Life, www.passiton.com/inspirational-sayings-billboards/15-determination-brooke-ellison. Accessed 1 May 2019.

Quinn, Helen, and Carole Flint. "The Technical Communication Resource Center and Writing Lab: Special Services for Basic, Technical, and Learning Disabled Writers." *The Writing Lab Newsletter*, vol. 14, no. 9, May 1990, pp. 10–14, wlnjournal.org/archives/v14/14-9.pdf.

Reid, Alex. "Portable Composition: iTunes University and Networked Pedagogies." *Computers and Composition*, vol. 25, no. 1, 2008, pp. 61–78, doi:10.1016/j.compcom.2007.09.003.

Rhodes, Jacqueline, and Jonathan Alexander. *Techne: Queer Meditations on Writing the Self.* Computers and Composition Digital Press, 2015.

Richards, Amy. "College Composition: Recognizing the Learning Disabled Writer." *The Journal of Basic Writing*, vol. 4, no. 2, Fall 1985, pp. 68–79, wac.colostate.edu/jbw/v4n2/richards.pdf. Accessed 15 July 2017.

Rinaldi, Kerri. "Disability in the Writing Center: A New Approach (That's Not So New)." *Praxis: A Writing Center Journal*, vol. 13, no. 1, 2015, www.praxisuwc.com/rinaldi-131. Accessed 15 July 2017.

Rose, Mike. "The Language of Exclusion: Writing Instruction at the University." *College English*, vol. 47, no. 4, Apr. 1985, pp. 341–59, doi:10.2307/376957.

Schmidt, Katherine, et al. "Lessening the Divide: Strategies for Promoting Effective Communication between Hearing Consultants and Deaf Student-Writers." *The Writing Lab Newsletter*, vol. 33, no. 5, Jan. 2009, pp. 6–10, wlnjournal.org/archives/v33/33.5.pdf.

Selber, Stuart A. *Multiliteracies for a Digital Age*. Southern Illinois UP, 2004.

———. "Reimagining the Functional Side of Computer Literacy." *College Composition and Communication*, vol. 55, no. 3, Feb. 2004, pp. 470–503, doi:10.2307/4140696.

Selfe, Cynthia L. "Technology and Literacy: A Story about the Perils of Not Paying Attention." *College Composition and Communication*, vol. 50, no. 3, Feb. 1999, pp. 411–36, doi:10.2307/358859.

Shapiro, Joseph P. *No Pity: People with Disabilities Forging a New Civil Rights Movement*. Three Rivers Press, 1994.

Shaughnessy, Mina P. *Errors and Expectations: A Guide for the Teacher of Basic Writing*. Oxford UP, 1977.

Sheridan, David M. "Writing Centers and the Multimodal Turn." Introduction. Sheridan and Inman, pp. 1–16.

Sheridan, David M., and James A. Inman, editors. *Multiliteracy Centers: Writing Center Work, New Media, and Multimodal Rhetoric*. Hampton Press, 2010.

Sherwood, Steve. "Apprenticed to Failure: Learning from the Students We Can't Help." *The Writing Center Journal*, vol. 17, no. 1, Fall 1996, pp. 49–57. *JSTOR*, www.jstor.org/stable/43442015.

Shipka, Jody. "Including, but Not Limited to, the Digital: Composing Multimodal Texts." *Multimodal Literacies and Emerging Genres*, edited by Tracey Bowen and Carl Whithaus, U of Pittsburgh P, 2013, pp. 73–89.

———. *Toward a Composition Made Whole*. U of Pittsburgh P, 2011.

Simpkins, Neil. "Towards an Understanding of Accommodation Transfer: Disabled Students' Strategies for Navigating Classroom Accommodations." *Composition Forum*, vol. 39, Summer 2018, compositionforum.com/issue/39/accommodation-transfer.php.

Stein, Pippa. *Multimodal Pedagogies in Diverse Classrooms: Representation, Rights and Resources*. Routledge, 2008.

"Threw Cancer a Curve Ball." *Pass It On*, The Foundation for a Better Life, https://www.passiton.com/inspirational-sayings-billboards/57-overcoming-adam-bender.

Titchkosky, Tanya. *The Question of Access: Disability, Space, Meaning*. U of Toronto P, 2011.

Towns, Cheryl Hofstetter. "Serving the Disabled in the Writing Center." *The Writing Lab Newsletter*, vol. 14, no. 3, Nov. 1989, pp. 14–16, wlnjournal.org/archives/v14/14-3.pdf. Accessed 15 July 2017.

Trimbur, John. "Multiliteracies, Social Futures, and Writing Centers." *The Writing Center Journal*, vol. 20, no. 2, Spring/Summer 2000, pp. 29–32. *JSTOR*, www.jstor.org/stable/43442098.

"The UDL Guidelines." *CAST.* udlguidelines.cast.org.

Vee, Annette, et al. "Podcasting the Writing Center: Notes on Design and Production." *The Writing Lab Newsletter*, vol. 34, no. 1, Sept. 2009, pp. 1–6, https://wlnjournal.org/archives/v34/34.1.pdf. Accessed 15 July 2017.

Vickers, Melana Zyla. "Accommodating College Students with Learning Disabilities: ADD, ADHD, and Dyslexia." *The James G. Martin Center for Academic Renewal*, March 2010, www.jamesgmartin.center/acrobat/vickers-mar2010.pdf. Accessed 15 July 2017.

Vidali, Amy. "Discourses of Disability and Basic Writing." Lewiecki-Wilson and Brueggemann, pp. 40–55.

Walters, Shannon. "Toward an Accessible Pedagogy: Dis/ability, Multimodality, and Universal Design in the Technical Communication Classroom." *Technical Communication Quarterly*, vol. 19, no. 4, 2010, pp. 427–54, doi:10.1080/10572252.2010.502090.

Weber, Rebecca A. "Perspectives: Insights from a Writing Center Lab Assistant." Babcock and Daniels, pp. 17–29.

Weitershausen, Inez von. "How to Stay Sane through a PhD: Get Survival Tips from Fellow Students." *The Guardian*, 20 Mar. 2014, www.theguardian.com/higher-education-network/blog/2014/mar/20/phd-research-mental-health-tips.

White, Linda Feldmeier. "Learning Disability, Pedagogies, and Public Discourse." *College Composition and Communication*, vol. 53, no. 4, June 2002, pp. 705–38, doi:10.2307/1512122.

Wilson, James C., and Cynthia Lewiecki-Wilson, editors. *Embodied Rhetorics: Disability in Language and Culture*. Southern Illinois UP, 2001.

Womack, Anne-Marie. "Teaching Is Accommodation: Universally Designing Composition Classrooms and Syllabi." *College Composition and Communication*, vol. 68, no. 3, Feb. 2017, pp. 494–525. *JSTOR*, www.jstor.org/stable/44783578.

Wood, Tara K. *Disability and College Composition: Investigating Access, Identity, and Rhetorics of Ableism*. 2014. U of Oklahoma, PhD dissertation.

———. "Overcoming Rhetoric: Forced Disclosure and the Colonizing Ethic of Evaluating Personal Essays." *Open Words Journal*, vol. 5, Spring 2011, pp. 38–52, wac.colostate.edu/docs/openwords/v5/wood.pdf. Accessed 15 July 2017.

———. "Rhetorical Disclosures: The Stakes of Disability Identity in Higher Education." Kerschbaum et al., pp. 75–92.
Wood, Tara, and Shannon Madden. "Suggested Practices for Syllabus Accessibility Statements." *Kairos: A Journal of Rhetoric, Technology, and Pedagogy*, vol. 18, no. 1, Fall 2013, kairos.technorhetoric.net/praxis/tiki-index.php?page=Suggested_Practices_for_Syllabus_Accessibility_Statements. Accessed 15 July 2017.
Wysocki, Anne Frances. "Into Between—On Composition in Mediation." Introduction. Arola and Wysocki, pp. 1–22.
Yergeau, Melanie. *Authoring Autism: On Rhetoric and Neurological Queerness*. Duke UP, 2018.
Yergeau, M. Remi, et al. "Expanding the Space of f2f: Writing Centers and Audio-Visual-Textual Conferencing." *Kairos: A Journal of Rhetoric, Technology, and Pedagogy*, vol. 13, no. 1, Fall 2008, technorhetoric.net/13.1/topoi/yergeau-et-al/. Accessed 15 July 2017.
Yergeau, M. Remi, et al. "Multimodality in Motion: Disability and Kairotic Spaces." *Kairos: A Journal of Rhetoric, Technology, and Pedagogy*, vol. 18, no. 1, Fall 2013, kairos.technorhetoric.net/18.1/coverweb/yergeau-et-al/. Accessed 15 July 2017.
Zdenek, Sean. "Accessible Podcasting: College Students on the Margins in the New Media Classroom." *Computers and Composition Online*, Fall 2009, seanzdenek.com/article-accessible-podcasting/. Accessed 15 July 2017.
———. *Reading Sounds: Closed-Captioned Media and Popular Culture*. U of Chicago P, 2015.
———. "Which Sounds Are Significant? Towards a Rhetoric of Closed Captioning." *Disability Studies Quarterly*, vol. 31, no. 3, 2011, dsq-sds.org/article/view/1667/1604/. Accessed 1 July 2017.
Zhang, Lingling, and Beth Haller. "Consuming Image: How Mass Media Impact the Identity of People with Disabilities." *Communication Quarterly*, vol. 61, no. 3, 2013, pp. 319–34, doi:10.1080/01463373.2013.776988.

INDEX

able-bodied, managing fears of the, 13, 18
ableism
  academic, 14–17
  defined, 93–94
  positioning disability, 94
Academic Ableism: Disability and Higher Education (Dolmage), 14, 19
accessibility
  as accommodation, 88–89
  collaborative, 57–59, 85–86
  culture of, creating a, 70, 128
  decision-makers, 36
  denials for, 4
  an ethical, rhetorical practice, 87–91
  listening for, 17, 128
  modeling, 126–27
  multimodal toolkits/strategies, 77–81
  requirements for, 17, 85–86
  retrofitting for, 19, 50, 88–89, 100, 119
  in writing studies research, 27–28
accessibility, functional and rhetorical
  alt text and image descriptions, 110–18
  audio transcription, 91–99
  captioning, 99–110
  collaborative note-taking, 86
"Accessible Podcasting" (Zdenek), 93
accommodations

absolving institutional responsibility, 19, 123
  as afterthoughts, 19, 88–89, 100, 119
  based on diagnostic criteria, 41–42
  disability statistics supporting, 5–6
  expectations accompanying, 41
  factors informing, 40
  for faculty, 2, 15, 34–35
  focus of, 41
  functional value of, 89–90
  positioning, 40–41
  purpose and goal of, 19
  reasonable, 2, 34–35, 40
  responsibilities accompanying, 41–42
accommodations, obtaining
  denied, 14–17
  disclosure requirement for, 22
  ease of, 1–4, 19–20
  power dynamics in, 40
  responsibility for, 89
accommodation through multimodal design
  alt text and image descriptions, 110–18
  captioning, 99–110
  transcription, 91–99
accommodation transfer, 41
agency
  erasure of, 65, 68
  UD for enabling, 74–77
agentive learning, promoting, 71–77

Alexander, Jonathan, 47, 116
alt text, 110–18
Americans with Disabilities Act (ADA), 35
anti-ableist futures, 59–60
"Apprenticed to Failure: Learning from the Students We Can't Help" (Sherwood), 67
"Articulating Betweenity: Literacy, Language, Identity, and Technology in the Deaf/Hard-of-Hearing Collection" (Brueggemann), 20–21, 101
Asperger's syndrome, 61, 69
attendance policies, 34
attention deficit disorder (ADD), 5–6
attention deficit hyperactivity disorder (ADHD), 5–6
audio, accessible, 91–99
audio-video-textual (AVT) conferencing, 73
Autism Speaks, 13–14
autism spectrum disorder, 5, 61, 69

Babcock, Rebecca Day, 62–63, 70–71, 78, 82
Bain, Zara, 16
"Becoming Visible: Lessons in Disability" (Brueggemann et al.), 43
belonging, 17
Bender, Adam, 11
Bérubé, Michael, 3
betweenity, 21, 102
Bowie, Jennifer, 93
Brilliant Imperfection (Clare), 1
Bruch, Patrick, 50
Brueggemann, Brenda, 20–21, 30, 43, 101–2, 106
Brueggemann, Karl, 102
Butler, Janine, 103

Campbell, Fiona Kumari, 93
cancer, 4, 9–10, 131nn4–6

captioning, 99–110
CAST, 49, 133n12
Claiming Disability: Knowledge and Identity (Linton), 3
Clare, Eli, 1
collaborative accessibility, 57–59, 85–86
college students. *See* higher education
Collins, Terry, 69
coming over
  engaging in a process of, requirements for, 21–22, 123–24
  meaning of, 20–21
  rhetorics of, 18–22
  in writing studies research and pedagogy, 22–28
composing practices, disabled
  legitimizing the rhetorical potential of, 52–59
  making space for, 43–44
  multimodal design for, 44–48, 57–58
  rhetorics of overcoming, resisting or reinforcing, 59–60
  strategies enabling, 54–59
  UD framework for, 48–52, 57–58
crip, term use, 132n7
culture of accessibility, 70, 88, 128
cure, overcoming as the backup plan for, 1, 7

Davidson, Cathy, 7, 58
Davis, Seth, 95
Deaf culture, 134nn20–21
decomposition, 56–57
deficit
  disability as, 37–40, 50, 128
  overcoming as, 20–21
Degner, Hillary, 80
De Mers, Kathleen Dunn, 49–50, 77
depression, 6
developmental disability, 5
difference
  collaboration by, 58–59

erasure of, 51–53
positioning disability as, 40–41, 51–53, 63, 66
Dinitz, Sue, 76–77
disability
  described, 3
  invisible, 28, 51–52
  IWCA position statement on, 81–82
  made visible, 2, 3–5, 10
  media's role in shaping cultural understandings of, 5, 11–14
  medicalized approaches to, 4–5, 7, 65–67
  reimagining education to accommodate, 7
  statistics, 5
  understanding, personal influences in, 3–5
disability, positioning
  ableism in, 94
  culturally, 5, 68
  as dangerous if undisclosed, 62
  as deficit, 37–40, 50, 128
  as difference, 40–41, 51–53, 63, 66, 94
  as failure, 41
  as inferiority, 8
"Dis/Ability in the Writing Center" (*Praxis*), 80
disability justice, 50, 127–28
disability research
  disclosure in, 31
  instructor workshop, 24–27
  methodological concerns, 23
  power dynamics in, 30
  self-reflexivity in, 30–31
  student study, 27–28
Disability Rhetoric (Dolmage), 18
disability social justice, 51
"Disability Studies Methodology: Explaining Ourselves to Ourselves" (Price), 30
disability studies within writing studies, 35

Disability Visibility (podcast) (Wong), 111, 114
disclosure
  in coming over, 123–24
  demands following, 3
  in disability research, 27–28, 29, 31
  by faculty, 1–3
  power dynamics of, 122
  required, 22, 80, 122–23
  risk management process in, 26
  risks of, 2, 14–15
  transformative, 124
  value of, 82–83
  weaponizing, 122
"Discourses of Disability and Basic Writing" (Vidali), 38
discrimination, disability-based, 4, 14–17
Dolmage, Jay, 10, 14, 18, 19, 34, 41, 46, 50
Dougherty, Tim, 111–12
Dunn, Patricia, 43, 49–50, 77, 133n11
dyslexia, 6, 12, 65–66

Ellis, Katie, 100
Ellison, Brooke, 12
environments, accessible. *See* universal design (UD)
Errors and Expectations: A Guide for the Teacher of Basic Writing (Shaughnessy), 37
ethics of accessibility, 48, 87–91, 119, 122–29
"Expanding the Space of f2f" (Yergeau et al.), 73

failure, disability as, 41
Feminist, Queer, Crip (Kafer), 12
Fishman, Teddi, 79
fitting in, 18–19, 38, 41, 89
Flint, Carole, 73
Foundation for a Better Life (FBL), 11–12

Garland-Thomson, Rosemarie, 3, 11
Garrison, Kristen, 9
Gleason, George, 65–66
Glenn, Cheryl, 94
Goldberg, Whoopi, 12
Grimm, Nancy, 75

Hamilton, Scott, 13
Hamraie, Aimi, 51
Harbour, Wendy, 131n3
#AcademicAbleism, 14–17, 19
Hawkes, Lory, 68–69
Hershey, Laura, 13
higher education
    academic ableism, 14–17, 19
    doctoral students, advice for, 16
    ethic of ability and perfection, 34
    expectations for overcoming, 17
    expectation to overcome, 38–39
    kairotic spaces of, 25–26, 28
    mental health services, demand for, 6
    student disability statistics, 5–6
    student mental health issues, 16
Horton, Sarah, 111
Howes, Franny, 48
"How to Stay Sane through a PhD: Get Survival Tips from Fellow Students" (*The Guardian*), 16

identity-first language, 131n1
images
    accessible, 110–18
    constructing understandings of disability, 11–13
inclusion
    accommodations for, 89
    responsibility for, 18–19, 41, 89
    in writing centers, 81–84
Individuals with Disabilities Education Act (IDEA), 68
inferiority, disability as, 8
infographics, 115–16
inhospitality, multimodal, 89

Inman, James, 75
inspirational discourses, 11–14
"Integrating Disability, Transforming Feminist Theory" (Garland-Thomson), 1–3
intellectual disability, 5
International Writing Centers Association (IWCA), 81–82
the invisible disabled, 28, 51–52
"'I Simply Gave Up Trying to Present at CCCC . . .'" (Dolmage et al.), 34

Jackson, Rebecca, 76

Kafer, Alison, 12–13
kairotic spaces, 25–26, 28
Kent, Mike, 100
Kerschbaum, Stephanie, 23, 25, 30–31, 89, 132n7
Kiedaisch, Jean, 76–77
"Knowing (Y)Our Story: Practicing Decolonial Rhetorical History" (Dougherty), 111–12
Konstant, Shoshana Beth, 78
Kopelson, Karen, 9
Kress, Gunther, 72

labeling, 7, 37
language, identity-first, 131n1
"Learning Disabilities and the Writing Center" (Neff), 67–68
learning disability scholarship, 39
learning disabled students, 65–68
Lewiecki-Wilson, Cynthia, 10
Linton, Simi, 3, 23
listening, 17, 128
literacy, functional and critical, 89
literacy narrative, overcoming the, 54

mad composing, 55–57
Madden, Shannon, 50
madness, mental health's conflation with, 15

Mann, April, 70
"Mapping Composition: Inviting Disability in the Front Door" (Dolmage), 50
McHarg, Molly, 80
McKee, Heidi, 91
McKinney, Jackie Grutsch, 76, 79
McRuer, Robert, 56, 132n7
media, constructing understandings of disability, 5, 11–14
medical model of disability, 4–5, 37–42, 65–67
mental health, student, 6, 16
"Mental Health: A University Crisis" (*The Guardian*), 16
mental illness, rhetorical dismissal of, 15
mind mapping, 54–56
Mingus, Mia, 127
multiliteracies, writing centers engaging, 71–74
Multiliteracies for a Digital Age (Selber), 89
multimodal design
  alt text and image descriptions, 110–18
  audio transcription, 91–99
  captioning, 99–110
  nondigital text example, 119
  potential of, 52–53
  purpose of, 45
  requirements for, 118
  toolkits and strategies, 77–81
"Multimodality in Motion" (Yergeau et al.), 48, 85, 88–89
multimodal literacies, writing centers engaging, 71–74
multimodal pedagogy
  composition and the nonnormative body, 43–48, 57–58
  privileging or excluding bodies, 46–48
multimodal practices
  beyond the classroom, 125–26
  as ethical, rhetorical practice, 87–91
  foregrounding, 118–21
  multiple literacy writing centers, 71–74
myths, common disability, 18

Nash, LeAnn, 134n21
National Park Service Instagram account, 115
Neff, Julie, 67–68
Netflix, 100
note-taking, collaborative, 86
Now You See It: How the Brain Science of Attention Will Transform the Way We Live, Work, and Learn (Davidson), 7

"A One-Woman Show with Elaine Richardson" (podcast), 95–97
On Multimodality: New Media in Composition Studies (Alexander & Rhodes), 47
"On Rhetorical Agency and Disclosing Disability in Academic Writing" (Kerschbaum), 25
overcoming
  as the backup plan for cure, 1, 7
  coming over vs., 20–22
  as deficit, 20–21
  expectations and demands for, 4–5, 7–9, 10–13, 17, 38–39, 57
  meaning of, 8
  myths of, 18
  as normalization, 57
  possibility of, 1
  responsibility for, 9–12, 19, 38–39
  shaping the culture of, 5, 11–14
overcoming discourses
  abelist society in positioning, 8
  academic ableism, examples of, 14–17
  communicating personal triumph, 8

empowering, 131n3
inspirational, 11–14
overcoming cancer, 9–10
purpose of, for the able-bodied, 13

Pemberton, Michael A., 61
personal narrative, 54
"Podcasting in a Writing Class? Considering the Possibilities" (Bowie), 93
podcasts, 46, 91–97, 135n27
Pratt, Mary Louise, 30
Price, Margaret, 15, 23, 25, 30, 132n7
Pryal, Katie Rose Guest, 15

Quesenbery, Whitney, 111
The Question of Access: Disability, Space, Meaning (Titchkosky), 17
Quinn, Helen, 73

Reading Sounds: Closed-Captioned Media and Popular Culture (Zdenek), 102–3
relationships, disability shaping, 3–5
retrofitting for accessibility, 19, 50, 88–89, 100
rhetoric, visual, 103–4
rhetorics of overcoming
  perpetuating, methods of, 66
  personal narrative in reinforcing the, 54
  positioning writers and embodiments as less than, 58–59
  reinforcing stigma of disability, 58–59
  resisting, methodology for, 29–31
  resisting, value in, 59–60, 124–25
  rewriting the, 18, 22
  rhetorics of coming over vs., 20–22
  social and cultural pervasiveness of, 14
Rhodes, Jacqueline, 47, 116
Richards, Amy, 39
Richardson, Elaine, 94–97

Selber, Stuart, 89–90
Selfe, Cynthia, 48, 87–88
"Serving the Disabled in the Writing Center" (Towns), 61, 70
Shaughnessy, Mina, 37
Sheridan, David, 72
Sherwood, Steve, 67
Shipka, Jody, 44–45, 47, 105
silence, 94
Simpkins, Neil, 41
sound, accessible, 91–99
"Sound Matters: Notes toward the Analysis and Design of Sound in Multimodal Webtexts" (McKee), 91
"'Special Needs' Students and Writing Centers" (Pemberton), 61
"Stories of Methodology: Interviewing Sideways, Crooked and Crip" (Price & Kerschbaum), 23
students, disabled
  inclusion, responsibility for, 18–19, 41, 89
  listening to, 17, 128
  supports for, well-intentioned, 59
student writers, disabled. *See also* composing practices, disabled
  accommodating, 40–42
  basic writers' relation to, 37–39
  diagnosing and remediating, 37–42, 65–67
success, overcoming conflated with, 14
super crips, 18
support animals, 2–3
syllabus, 50–51

teacher training, 27–28
Techne: Queer Meditations on Writing the Self (Rhodes & Alexander), 116
technology
  creating opportunity through, 46–47
  privileging or excluding bodies, 46

taking responsibility for required use of, 88
in writing centers, 72–74
"Technology and Literacy: A Story about the Perils of Not Paying Attention" (Selfe), 87–88
Tell Me How It Reads: Tutoring Deaf and Hearing Students in the Writing Center (Babcock), 62–63, 70–71
This Rhetorical Life (podcast), 92, 95
Titchkosky, Tanya, 17, 67
Toward a Composition Made Whole (Shipka), 44–45
Toward a New Rhetoric of Difference (Kerschbaum), 30–31
Towns, Cheryl Hofstetter, 61, 70
transcription, 91–99, 102–3
Trimbur, John, 71, 73
tropes, common disability, 18
tutoring, online, 73
Twitter feeds, on denial of access to accommodations, 16–17

universal design (UD)
beyond the classroom, 126
erasing material needs, 86
in writing centers, 74–77, 83
in writing classrooms, 48–53, 57–58
universal design for learning (UDL), 49, 133n12

Vidali, Amy, 38
video, accessible, 99–110
visual content, accessing
alt text and image descriptions, 110–18
captioning, 99–110

Walters, Shannon, 40
A Web for Everyone: Designing Accessible User Experiences (Horton & Quesenbery), 111

"Which Sounds Are Significant? Towards a Rhetoric of Closed Captioning" (Zdenek), 102
White, Linda Feldmeier, 41, 42
Womack, Anne-Marie, 51
Wong, Alice, 111, 112, 114–15
Wood, Tara, 50, 54
writers, basic
disabled writers relation to, 37–39
expectations to overcome, 38–39
"Writing against Normal: Navigating a Corporeal Turn" (Dolmage), 46
writing centers
accommodation practices, 67–71
agency, erasure of, 68
agentive learning, promoting, 71–77
coming over, process of, 82
common practices, 62–63
culture of accessibility, shifting the, 70
diagnostic and remediation approaches, 65–67
environmental design moving beyond diagnosis, 83
functions of, 62
inclusion, moving toward, 81–84
learning disabilities in, 65–68
legal obligations, 68–69
multimodal toolkits/strategies, 77–81
multiple literacies, supporting, 71–74
physical spaces of, 74–75
positioning students, 63
remedial labeling of, 62
rhetorics of overcoming, perpetuating, 64–71
tutor training, 70–71, 76
universal design (UD) in, 74–77, 83
writing classrooms. *See also* composing practices, disabled
accommodations in, 41

medical model of disability in, 37–42
multimodal framework, 44–48, 57–58
as remedial spaces, 37
universal design (UD) for, 48–53
writing studies
coming over in, 22–28

disability studies informing, 35
reimagining, 124–25
remediation models in, 38

Yergeau, M. Remi, 73, 85, 88–89
YouTube, 99

Zdenek, Sean, 93, 102–3, 111

AUTHOR

Allison Harper Hitt is assistant professor of rhetoric and composition at Ball State University. She teaches a range of writing courses, including professional writing and editing, digital literacies, and composition pedagogy. Hitt's educational backgrounds in cultural rhetorics and disability studies influence her commitments to developing pedagogical environments that affirm students' embodiments and provide multiple access points for engagement and rhetorical expression. Her research focuses on how disability is constructed, mediated, and contested within institutional systems. More specifically, she is interested in whose stories and bodies are valued within cultural and disciplinary histories and how instructors can collaborate with students to theorize and enact more socially just pedagogical practices. Her work has been published in *Business and Professional Communication Quarterly, Composition Forum, Rhetoric Review, The Oxford Guide for Writing Tutors: Practice and Research,* and *Praxis: A Writing Center Journal.*

BOOKS IN THE CCCC STUDIES IN WRITING & RHETORIC SERIES

Rhetorics of Overcoming: Rewriting Narratives of Disability and Accessibility in Writing Studies
Allison Harper Hitt

Writing Accomplices with Student Immigrant Rights Organizers
Glenn Hutchinson

Counterstory: The Rhetoric and Writing of Critical Race Theory
Aja Y. Martinez

Writing Programs, Veterans Studies, and the Post-9/11 University: A Field Guide
D. Alexis Hart and Roger Thompson

Beyond Progress in the Prison Classroom: Options and Opportunities
Anna Plemons

Rhetorics Elsewhere and Otherwise: Contested Modernities, Decolonial Visions
Edited by Romeo García and Damián Baca

Black Perspectives in Writing Program Administration: From the Margins to the Center
Edited by Staci M. Perryman-Clark and Collin Lamont Craig

Translanguaging outside the Academy: Negotiating Rhetoric and Healthcare in the Spanish Caribbean
Rachel Bloom-Pojar

Collaborative Learning as Democratic Practice: A History
Mara Holt

Reframing the Relational: A Pedagogical Ethic for Cross-Curricular Literacy Work
Sandra L. Tarabochia

Inside the Subject: A Theory of Identity for the Study of Writing
Raúl Sánchez

Genre of Power: Police Report Writers and Readers in the Justice System
Leslie Seawright

Assembling Composition
Edited by Kathleen Blake Yancey and Stephen J. McElroy

Public Pedagogy in Composition Studies
Ashley J. Holmes

From Boys to Men: Rhetorics of Emergent American Masculinity
Leigh Ann Jones

Freedom Writing: African American Civil Rights Literacy Activism, 1955–1967
Rhea Estelle Lathan

The Desire for Literacy: Writing in the Lives of Adult Learners
Lauren Rosenberg

On Multimodality: New Media in Composition Studies
Jonathan Alexander and Jacqueline Rhodes

Toward a New Rhetoric of Difference
Stephanie L. Kerschbaum

Rhetoric of Respect: Recognizing Change at a Community Writing Center
Tiffany Rousculp

After Pedagogy: The Experience of Teaching
Paul Lynch

Redesigning Composition for Multilingual Realities
Jay Jordan

Agency in the Age of Peer Production
Quentin D. Vieregge, Kyle D. Stedman, Taylor Joy Mitchell, and Joseph M. Moxley

Remixing Composition: A History of Multimodal Writing Pedagogy
Jason Palmeri

First Semester: Graduate Students, Teaching Writing, and the Challenge of Middle Ground
Jessica Restaino

Agents of Integration: Understanding Transfer as a Rhetorical Act
Rebecca S. Nowacek

Digital Griots: African American Rhetoric in a Multimedia Age
Adam J. Banks

The Managerial Unconscious in the History of Composition Studies
Donna Strickland

Everyday Genres: Writing Assignments across the Disciplines
Mary Soliday

The Community College Writer: Exceeding Expectations
Howard Tinberg and Jean-Paul Nadeau

A Taste for Language: Literacy, Class, and English Studies
James Ray Watkins

Before Shaughnessy: Basic Writing at Yale and Harvard, 1920–1960
Kelly Ritter

Writer's Block: The Cognitive Dimension
Mike Rose

Teaching/Writing in Thirdspaces: The Studio Approach
Rhonda C. Grego and Nancy S. Thompson

Rural Literacies
Kim Donehower, Charlotte Hogg, and Eileen E. Schell

Writing with Authority: Students' Roles as Writers in Cross-National Perspective
David Foster

Whistlin' and Crowin' Women of Appalachia: Literacy Practices since College
Katherine Kelleher Sohn

Sexuality and the Politics of Ethos in the Writing Classroom
Zan Meyer Gonçalves

African American Literacies Unleashed: Vernacular English and the Composition Classroom
Arnetha F. Ball and Ted Lardner

Revisionary Rhetoric, Feminist Pedagogy, and Multigenre Texts
Julie Jung

Archives of Instruction: Nineteenth-Century Rhetorics, Readers, and Composition Books in the United States
Jean Ferguson Carr, Stephen L. Carr, and Lucille M. Schultz

Response to Reform: Composition and the Professionalization of Teaching
Margaret J. Marshall

Multiliteracies for a Digital Age
Stuart A. Selber

Personally Speaking: Experience as Evidence in Academic Discourse
Candace Spigelman

Self-Development and College Writing
Nick Tingle

Minor Re/Visions: Asian American Literacy Narratives as a Rhetoric of Citizenship
Morris Young

A Communion of Friendship: Literacy, Spiritual Practice, and Women in Recovery
Beth Daniell

Embodied Literacies: Imageword and a Poetics of Teaching
Kristie S. Fleckenstein

Language Diversity in the Classroom: From Intention to Practice
Edited by Geneva Smitherman and Victor Villanueva

Rehearsing New Roles: How College Students Develop as Writers
Lee Ann Carroll

Across Property Lines: Textual Ownership in Writing Groups
Candace Spigelman

Mutuality in the Rhetoric and Composition Classroom
David L. Wallace and Helen Rothschild Ewald

The Young Composers: Composition's Beginnings in Nineteenth-Century Schools
Lucille M. Schultz

Technology and Literacy in the Twenty-First Century: The Importance of Paying Attention
Cynthia L. Selfe

Women Writing the Academy: Audience, Authority, and Transformation
Gesa E. Kirsch

Gender Influences: Reading Student Texts
Donnalee Rubin

Something Old, Something New: College Writing Teachers and Classroom Change
Wendy Bishop

Dialogue, Dialectic, and Conversation: A Social Perspective on the Function of Writing
Gregory Clark

Audience Expectations and Teacher Demands
Robert Brooke and John Hendricks

Toward a Grammar of Passages
Richard M. Coe

Rhetoric and Reality: Writing Instruction in American Colleges, 1900–1985
James A. Berlin

Writing Groups: History, Theory, and Implications
Anne Ruggles Gere

Teaching Writing as a Second Language
Alice S. Horning

Invention as a Social Act
Karen Burke LeFevre

The Variables of Composition: Process and Product in a Business Setting
Glenn J. Broadhead and Richard C. Freed

Writing Instruction in Nineteenth-Century American Colleges
James A. Berlin

Computers & Composing: How the New Technologies Are Changing Writing
Jeanne W. Halpern and Sarah Liggett

A New Perspective on Cohesion in Expository Paragraphs
Robin Bell Markels

Evaluating College Writing Programs
Stephen P. Witte and Lester Faigley

This book was typeset in Garamond and Frutiger by Barbara Frazier.
Typefaces used on the cover include Garamond and News Gothic.
The book was printed on 50-lb. White Offset paper
by Seaway Printing Company, Inc.

www.ingramcontent.com/pod-product-compliance
Lightning Source LLC
Chambersburg PA
CBHW060955230426
43665CB00015B/2209